Street by Street

IPSWICH

FELIXSTOWE, HADLEIGH, NEEDHAM MARKET, WOODBRIDGE

Bramford, Capel St Mary, Great Blakenham, Grundisburgh, Kesgrave, Kirton, Martlesham, Martlesham Heath, Sproughton, Trimley St Mary, Washbrook

1st edition February 2003

Published by AA Publishing (a trading name of Automobile Association Developments Limited, whose registered office is Millstream, Maidenhead Road, Windsor, Berkshire SL4 5GD. Registered number 1878835).

The Post Office is a registered trademark of Post Office Ltd. in the UK and other countries. Schools address data provided by Education Direct. One-way street data provided by:

Tele Atlas © Tele Atlas N.V.

Mapping produced by the Cartographic Department of The Automobile Association. A01553

A CIP Catalogue record for this book is available from the British Library.
Printed by GRAFIASA S.A., Porto, Portugal
The contents of this atlas are believed to be correct at the time of the latest revision. However, the publishers cannot be held responsible for loss occasioned to any person acting or refraining from action as a result of any material in this atlas, nor for any errors, omissions or changes in such material. This does not affect your statutory rights. The publishers would welcome information to correct any errors or omissions and to keep this atlas up to date. Please write to Publishing, The Automobile Association, Fanum House (FH17), Basing View, Basingstoke, Hampshire, RG21 4EA.

Ref: ML143

Key to map pages ii-iii

Key to map symbols iv-1

Enlarged scale pages 2-3

Street by Street 4-47

Index – towns & villages 48

Index – streets 49-55

Index – featured places 56-57

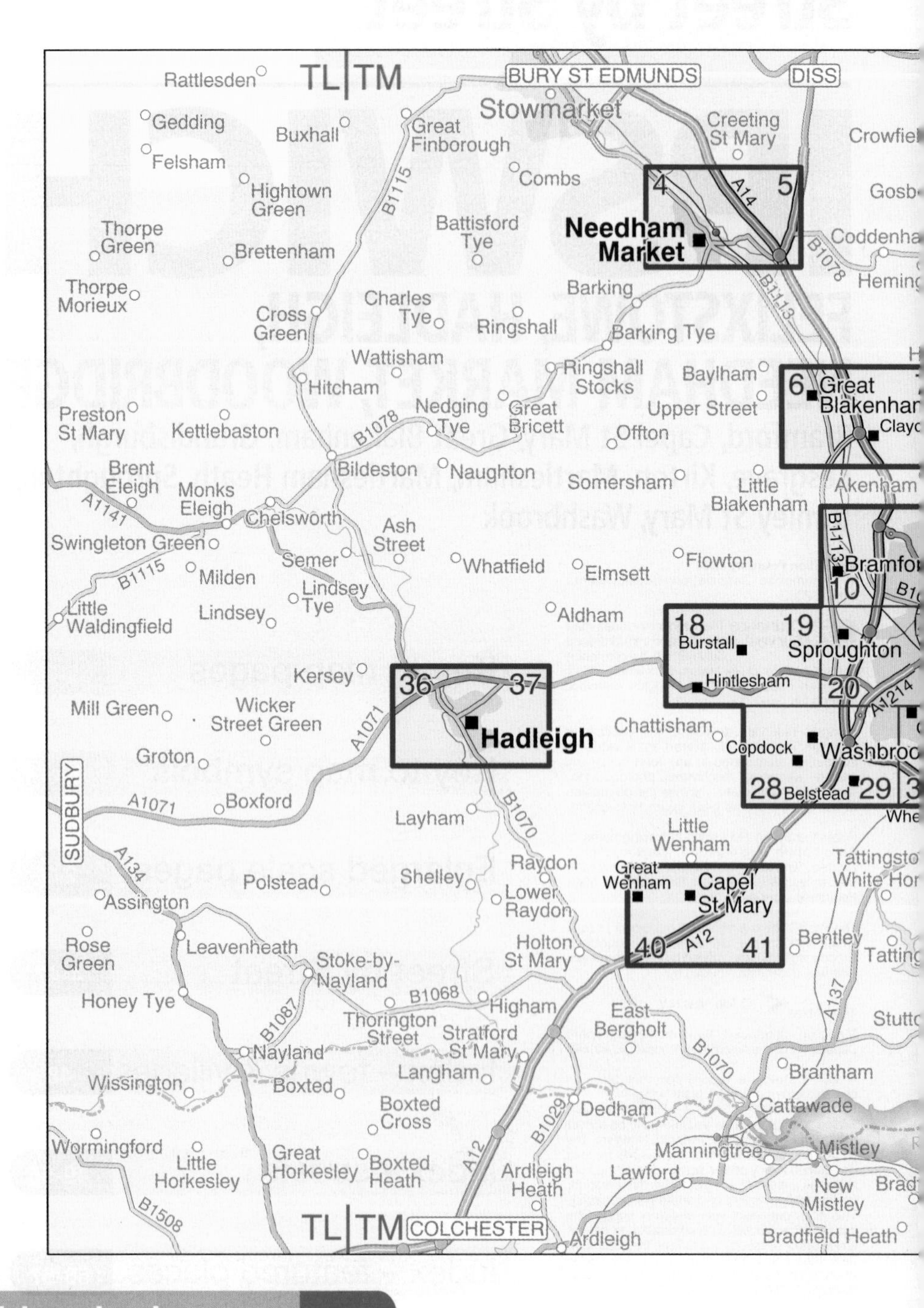

Enlarged scale pages **1:10,000** **6.3 inches to 1 mile**

0 — 1/4 — miles — 1/2

0 — 1/4 — 1/2 — kilometres — 3/4 — 1

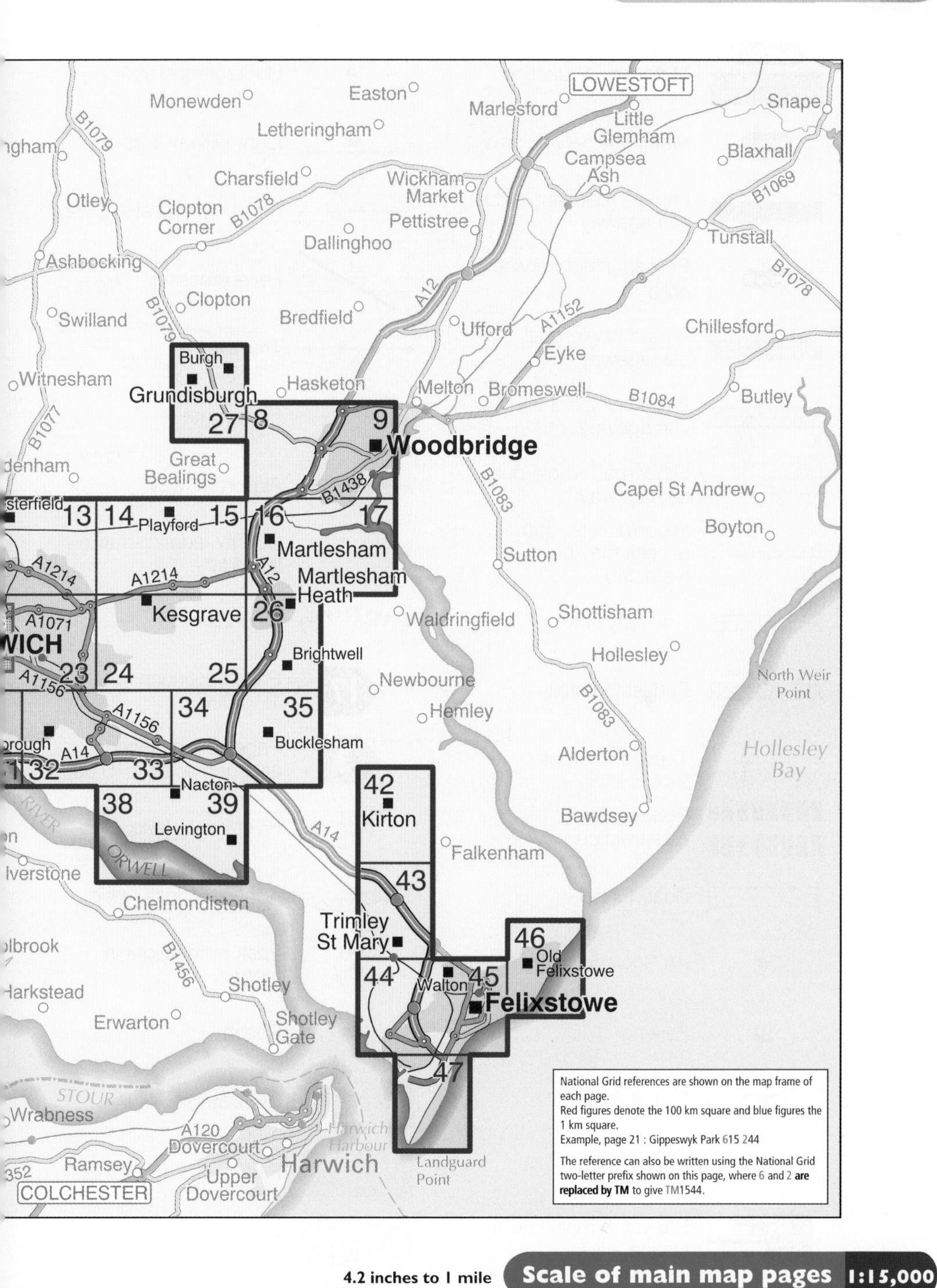

National Grid references are shown on the map frame of each page.
Red figures denote the 100 km square and blue figures the 1 km square.
Example, page 21 : Gippeswyk Park 615 244

The reference can also be written using the National Grid two-letter prefix shown on this page, where 6 and 2 **are replaced by TM** to give TM1544.

4.2 inches to 1 mile

Scale of main map pages 1:15,000

0 1/4 miles 1/2 3/4 1

0 1/4 1/2 kilometres 3/4 1 1 1/4 1 1/2

Junction 9 — Motorway & junction

Services — Motorway service area

Primary road single/dual carriageway

Services — Primary road service area

A road single/dual carriageway

B road single/dual carriageway

Other road single/dual carriageway

Minor/private road, access may be restricted

One-way street

Pedestrian area

Track or footpath

Road under construction

Road tunnel

AA — AA Service Centre

P — Parking

P+ — Park & Ride

Bus/coach station

Railway & main railway station

Railway & minor railway station

Underground station

Light railway & station

Preserved private railway

LC — Level crossing

Tramway

Ferry route

Airport runway

County, administrative boundary

Mounds

17 — Page continuation 1:15,000

3 — Page continuation to enlarged scale 1:10,000

River/canal, lake, pier

Aqueduct, lock, weir

465 Winter Hill — Peak (with height in metres)

Beach

Woodland

Park

Cemetery

Built-up area

Symbol	Meaning	Symbol	Meaning
	Featured building		Abbey, cathedral or priory
	City wall		Castle
A&E	Hospital with 24-hour A&E department		Historic house or building
PO	Post Office	Wakehurst Place NT	National Trust property
	Public library	M	Museum or art gallery
i	Tourist Information Centre		Roman antiquity
	Petrol station Major suppliers only		Ancient site, battlefield or monument
	Church/chapel		Industrial interest
	Public toilets		Garden
	Toilet with disabled facilities		Arboretum
PH	Public house AA recommended		Farm or animal centre
	Restaurant AA inspected		Zoological or wildlife collection
	Theatre or performing arts centre		Bird collection
	Cinema		Nature reserve
	Golf course	V	Visitor or heritage centre
	Camping AA inspected		Country park
	Caravan Site AA inspected		Cave
	Camping & caravan site AA inspected		Windmill
	Theme park		Distillery, brewery or vineyard

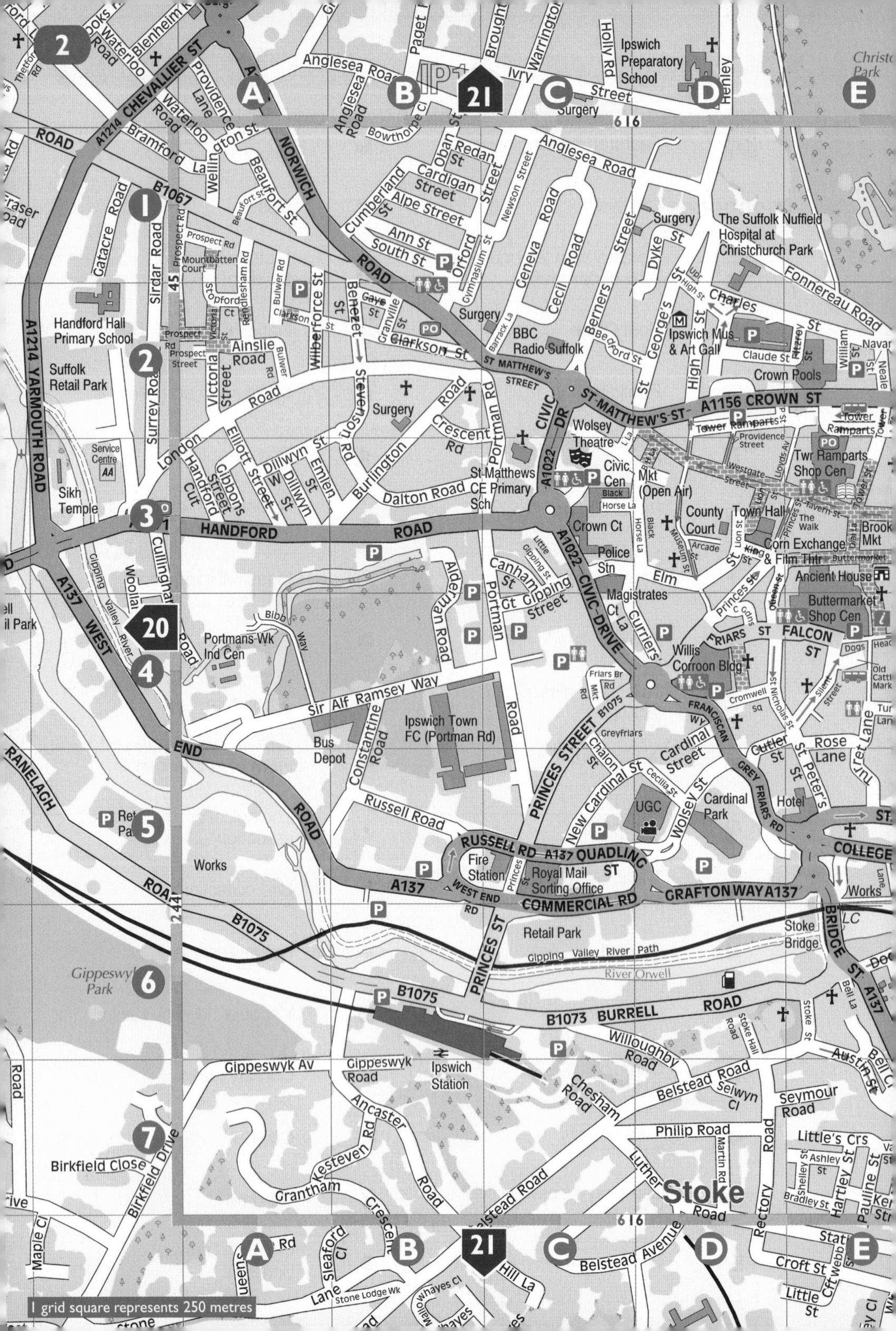

2
A
B
C
D
E
21
20
1
2
3
4
5
6
7
616
45
244
Waterloo Road
Blenheim Rd
Providence Lane
Anglesea Road
Paget Rd
Broughton Rd
Warrington Rd
Ivry Street
Holly Rd
Ipswich Preparatory School
Henley Rd
Christchurch Park
Surgery
A1214 CHEVALLIER ST
NORWICH ROAD
Bramford Road
Bramford La
Wellington St
Beaufort St
Bowthorpe Cl
Oban St
Redan St
Cardigan Street
Cumberland St
Alpe Street
Ann St
South St
Orford St
Gymnasium St
Newson Street
Geneva Road
Cecil Road
Berners Street
Dyke St
The Suffolk Nuffield Hospital at Christchurch Park
Fonnereau Road
Fraser Road
Catacre Road
Sirdar Road
B1067
Prospect Rd
Mountbatten Court
Rendlesham Rd
Bulwer Rd
Wilberforce St
Benezet St
Gaye St
Granville St
Clarkson St
Surgery
Barrack La
BBC Radio Suffolk
Bedford St
St George's St
Ipswich Mus. & Art Gall
High St
Upr High St
Charles St
Claude St
Fitzroy St
William St
Navarre St
Neale St
Crown Pools
Handford Hall Primary School
Suffolk Retail Park
Ainslie Road
Victoria Street
Bulwer Rd
ST MATTHEW'S STREET
ST MATTHEW'S ST
A1156 CROWN ST
Tower Ramparts
Providence Street
Lloyds Av
Westgate Street
Twr Ramparts Shop Cen
Tavern St
Tower St
Surrey Road
London Road
Stevenson Rd
Surgery
Crescent Rd
Burlington Road
Portman Rd
CIVIC DR
A1022
Wolsey Theatre
Civic Cen
Mkt (Open Air)
St Matthews CE Primary Sch
Dalton Road
Dillwyn St
Emlen St
Elliott Street
Gibbons Street
Handford Cut
Handford Road
Service Centre
AA
Sikh Temple
Cullingham Road
HANDFORD ROAD
Black Horse La
Crown Ct
County Court
Town Hall
The Walk
Corn Exchange & Film Thtr
Buttermarket
Brook Mkt
Museum St
Arcade St
Lion St
King St
Police Stn
Elm St
Ancient House
Buttermarket Shop Cen
A1022 CIVIC DRIVE
Little Gipping St
Canham St
Gt Gipping Street
Alderman Road
Magistrates Ct
Curriers' La
Princes St
Queen St
FRIARS ST
FALCON ST
Dogs Head St
Old Cattle Mark
Silent Street
Turret Lane
A137 WEST END ROAD
A1214 YARMOUTH ROAD
Gipping Valley River Path
Woollards Cl
Bibb Way
Portmans-Wk Ind Cen
Willis Corroon Bldg
Friars Br Rd
Friars Mkt Rd
Sir Alf Ramsey Way
Ipswich Town FC (Portman Rd)
Bus Depot
Constantine Road
B1075
PRINCES STREET
Greyfriars
Chalon St
New Cardinal St
Cecilia St
Cardinal Street
Wolsey St
FRANCISCAN WY
GREY FRIARS RD
Cromwell Sq
Nicholas St
St Peter's St
Cutler St
Rose Lane
Hotel
Cardinal Park
UGC
RANELAGH ROAD
Retail Park
Russell Road
RUSSELL RD A137 QUADLING ST
Fire Station
Royal Mail Sorting Office
COMMERCIAL RD
GRAFTON WAY A137
COLLEGE ST
Lane
Works
Works
Retail Park
B1075
Stoke Bridge
BRIDGE ST A137
LC
Gippeswyk Park
Gipping Valley River Path
River Orwell
B1075
B1073 BURRELL ROAD
Bell La
Stoke St
Austin St
Ipswich Station
Gippeswyk Av
Gippeswyk Road
Willoughby Road
Stoke Hall Road
Chesham Road
Belstead Road
Selwyn Cl
Seymour Road
Ancaster Rd
Kesteven Rd
Philip Road
Martin Rd
Luther Road
Rectory Road
Little's Crs
Ashley St
Shelley St
Hartley St
Pauline St
Bradley St
Birkfield Close
Birkfield Drive
Grantham Crescent
Belstead Road
Stoke
Road
Road
Maple Cl
Queens
Sleaford Cl
Stone Lodge Wk
Lane
Hill La
Belstead Avenue
Croft St
Webb St
Little Croft St
Station St
1 grid square represents 250 metres

IPSWICH
IP4
IP3
Woodbridge Road
Albion Hill
St Helen's St
Foxhall Road
Grove Lane
Fore Street A1156
Fore Hamlet
A1156 Bishop's Hill
Duke Street
Cliff Road
Back Hamlet
Cavendish Street
Spring Road
Alexandra Park
Suffolk College
Council Building
County Hall
Register Office
Regent Thtr
Odeon
Surgery
St Helens Primary Sch
St Margarets CE Primary School
St Marys Catholic Primary School
Clifford Rd Primary Sch
Blackfriars Priory Hall
Fore St Pool
Salvation Army
Old Customs House
Wet Dock
Holywells Park
Works
Rose Hill

Creeting Hall
Gipping Valley River Path
Grove Farm
Mill Lane
Church Lane
A
B
C
D
608
09
River Gipping
Jack's Green
Church Lane
A14
Watering Farm
STOWMARKET ROAD
B1113
BADLEY HILL
Badley Hill
Jordan Cl
Gipping Valley River Path
St Mary's Road
Road
St Mary's Gdns
LC
Gipsy La
Freehold Rd
Hill House Lane
Steggall Cl
Hill House Farm
Ludbrook Cl
Meadow Vw
Luff Meadow
Orchard Ga
Anderson Cl
Hurstlea Road
Council Building
Hawks Mill St
Needham Market
Crown St
Burton Dr
Paget Cl
Alexander Dr
Gilbert Cl
Platten Cl
Bridge St
The Pightle
PO
Park Road
Theobald Cl
HIGH STREET
Crowley Rd
Priestly Rd
Quinton Rd
Lane
Barrett's
Cem
The Causeway
School St
Needham Market Station
Pump St
Station Yd
CODDENHAM
Bosmere Primary School
Needham Market Middle School
IPSWICH ROAD
B1078
Road
Morris Wy
Jcksn Wy
Chainhouse Rd
Pinecroft Wy
Limetree Cl
Lion La
Lupin Wy
Primrose Avenue
Grinstead Gdns
Grinstead Hill
Clover Cl
Orchd Wy
Lilac Wk
Foxglove Avenue
Cwslp Wy
Rose Wk
Hargrave
BARKING ROAD
Chalkeith Rd
Surgery
Grinstead Hill
1
2
3
4
5
56
55
254
1 grid square represents 500 metres

Creeting St Mary
Primary School
Creeting
St Mary
E
F
G
H
10
11
Holt's Lane
Holt's Lane
Holt's Lane
A140
56
Coddenham
Green
2
Buck's Head Lane
I
A14
Sally Wood's Lane
3
Flordon Road
55
Hungercut
Hall
B1078
CODDENHAM RD
Coddenham Road
4
Needham
Lake
KETTLE LANE
Bosmere
Hall
A140
Cipping Valley River Path
Williamsport Way
Wilmsprt Wy
Lion Barn
Industrial
Est
B1113
A14
5
254
Long
Covert
Pipps
Ford

A
B
C
D
1
2
3
4
5
611
12
51
50
249
Gipping Valley River Path
STOWMARKET ROAD
Norwich Road
Sandy
A14
Maple Cv
Lower Crescent
The Crescent
Pesthouse Lane
Great Blakenham
Gipping Valley River Path
Chequers Rise
Kingfisher Dr
Mill Lane
Chalk Hill Lane
Cem
Hood Dr
Wnwt Gdns
Keytes Way
B1113
Stowmarket Rd
Aspen Cl
Laurel Dr
Mulberry Gdns
Plummers Dell
Works
Claydon Business Park
Gipping Road
LC
Bridge Trading Estate
Mas Ct
Fltchr
Coopers
Frst
Statn
BRAMFORD ROAD
Column Field Quarry
Chapel Lane
Barn La
Blue
Addison Wy
New Industrial Site
Lodge La
Council Building
Cottage Farm
Blackacre Hill
BRAMFORD ROAD B1113
River Gipping
Broomvale Farm
Broomvale Business Centre
The Common
Little Blakenham
The Beeches
Lane
Pound
1 grid square represents 500 metres

E
F
G
H
Harvey's Lane
14
15
Mill
Cooper's Road
Barham
IP6
Church Lane
Manor Farm
I
2
3
4
5
51
50
249
Church Lane
Old Rectory Cl
Thornhill
Glebe Wy
Winchester Gardens
Phillipps Rd
Mdtn Rd
Eddowes Rd
Ely Rd
Lincoln Gdns
Beacon Road
Bacon Rd
Edinburgh Gardens
Road
Exeter Rd
Jubilee Close
York
Lancaster Way
Claydon Primary School
Claydon
The Slade
High House Farm
Rede Lane
Rede Lane
The Knole
Highfield Dr
Back Lane
Crescent
Claydon High School
Church Lane
Church Lane
Church Lane
Church Lane
PO
Hotel
Drury Rd
Chestnut Dr
Poplar Cl
Laurel Wy
Hall La
Newell Rise
Hazel Rise
The Beeches
Willow Cl
Old
Ipswich Road
Works
Bower Farm
Hill View Business
Rise Hall
Akenham
Mockbeggars Hall

Works
Water La
Low Road
Top Rd
Boulge
Hasketon
Home Farm
Tymmes Pl
IP13
Mill Lane
Riverside
Church Road
Shrubbery Road
Pinners Lane
GRUNDISBURGH RD
27
B1079
GRUNDISBURGH ROAD
Bealings Lane
Hasketon Grange
Yew Tree House
Manor Road
Works
Rosery Lane
Bealings House
Seckford Hall
Golf Course
Rosery Farm
Lodge Road
St Peter's Cl
St Annes Cl
Oxford Drive
Christchurch Drive
Trinity Cl
Seckford Hall Rd
Hotel
Seckford Golf Centre
A12
Borrett Pl
Clayton Ct
Fynn Rd
Crane Cl
IPSWICH
Fynn Valley
16
B1438
Brock Lane
Top St
1 grid square represents 500 metres

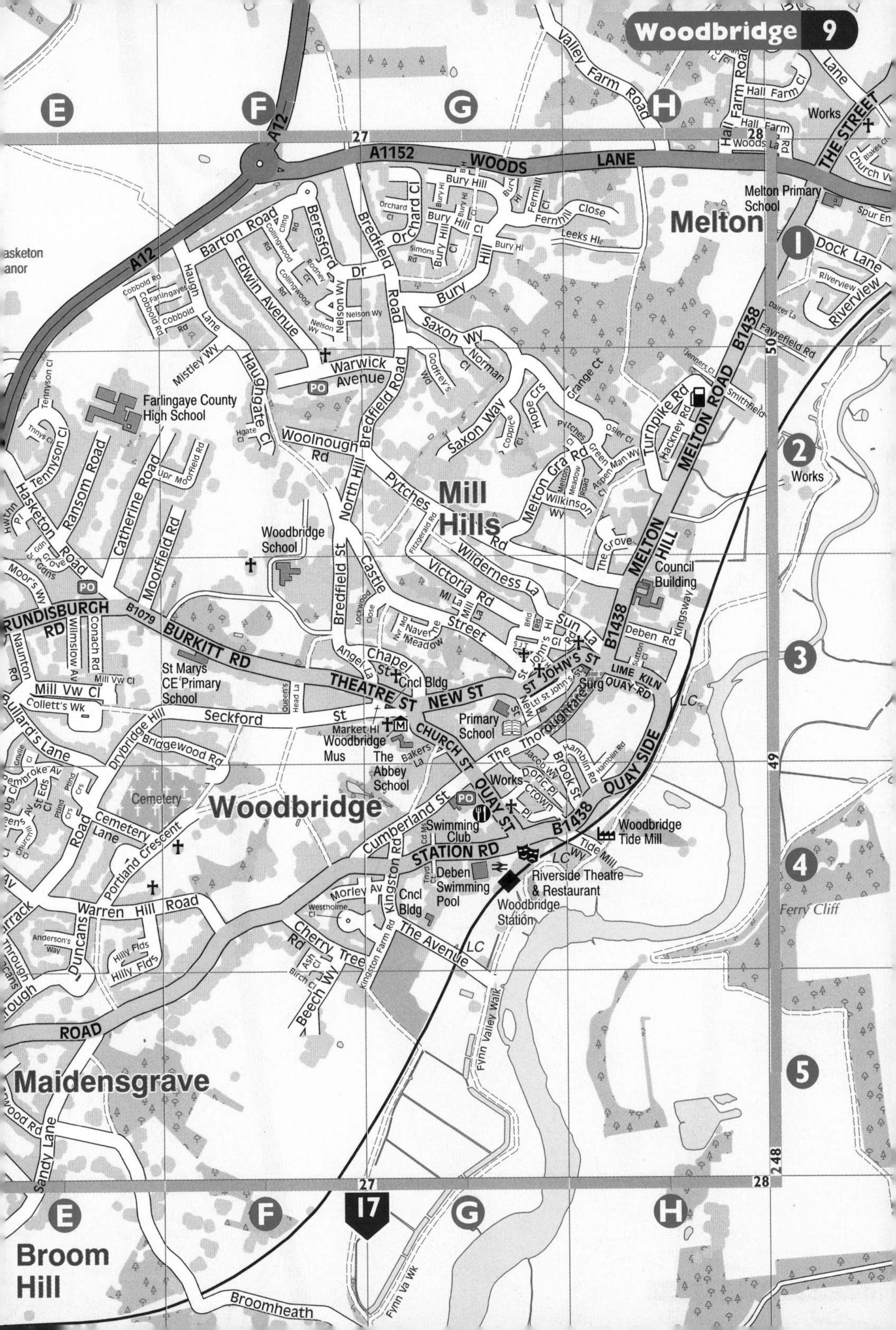
Melton
Mill Hills
Woodbridge
Maidensgrave
Broom Hill
A12
A1152 WOODS LANE
B1438
B1079
BURKITT RD
THEATRE ST
NEW ST
CHURCH ST
QUAY ST
STATION RD
QUAY SIDE
MELTON ROAD
MELTON HILL
ST JOHN'S ST
LIME KILN QUAY RD
THE STREET
Farlingaye County High School
Woodbridge School
St Marys CE Primary School
Primary School
The Abbey School
Woodbridge Mus
Council Building
Melton Primary School
Woodbridge Tide Mill
Riverside Theatre & Restaurant
Woodbridge Station
Deben Swimming Pool
Swimming Club
Cemetery
Ferry Cliff
Works
17

Suffolk Water Park
The Common
Works
Woodlands Way
BURY RD
Meadows West
Superstore
Whit
River Gipping
Gipping Va River Path
Grove House
Goddard Road
Whitehouse Industrial Estate
Goddard Rd East
White House
Paper Mill Lane
Hillcrest Ap
Hibbard Road
Limes Av
Whitton Leyer
A14(T)
Olympus Close
Wicklow Rd
Donegal Road
Kildare Av
Crossley Gdns
Foden Avenue
Maudslay Road
Daimler Rd
Lovetofts Drive
Kerry
Wexford Road
Connaught Rd
Antrim Road
Kerry Av
Lagonda Drive
Riley Cl
Bentley Rd
Morgan Cl
Lotus
Drive
Ulster Av
Agate Cl
Coral Drive
Diamond Close
High View Road
Opal Av
Pearl Road
Henniker
BRAMFORD ROAD
Adair Rd
Weaver Cl
Spinner Close
Lone Barn Ct
PO
Europa Way
Farthing Rd
Sproughton Business Park
Farthing Road Industrial Estate
Road
B1113
LORAINE WAY
Cutters Farm
B1067
THE STREET
Cem
Acton Road
Acton Rd
Acton Gdns
Fraser
Chapel Field
Acton Close
Flindell Dr
Broke Avenue
Mill Fld
Road
Bramford
Bullen Close
Bullen Lane
Lacon Rd
Leggatt Dr
Gipping Way
Ravens Lane
Angel Rd
Orchard Road
Packard Pl
Mill La
Bullen Lane
Gippingstone Rd
SHIP LANE
Bramford CE Primary Sch
Church Gn
Duckamere
St Mary's Cl
Vicarage Lane
Fitzgerald Road
Vicarage Close
Loraine Way
B1067
Thornbush Hall
Thornbush La
Runcton Farm
Sproughton Manor
Walk
Grindle Farm
The Grindle
612
13
48
47
246
A
B
C
D
1
2
3
4
5
20
1 grid square represents 500 metres

Bramford 11
Thurleston Lane
E
F
G
H
15
16
48
47
246
Sparrowe's Nest
I
2
3
4
5
12
21
Goodwood Close
Epsom
Drive
Henley Rd
Henley Road
Lambourne Rd
Ludlow Close
Taunton Close
Chpstw Rd
Lingfield Rd
Mitford Close
Thurleston County High School
Carlyle Cl
Homer Close
Whitton Church Lane
Byron Road
Hardy Cres
Defoe Road
Maycroft Close
Sandown Road
Lincoln Cl
Lincoln Close
Henley Avenue
Ballater Close
Shakespeare
Goldsmith Road
Thackeray Road
Chaucer Rd
Spenser Road
Kt Cl
Macaulay Road
Parnell Close
Parnell
Heathercroft Rd
Hzl Rd
L Cl
Shenstone Drive
Hollycroft Cl
Dryden Road
Kempton Cl
Kempton Rd
PO
Thomas Wolsey Special Sch
Whitton Community Primary School
Blake Road
Browning Road
Kipling Rd
Coleridge Rd
Moore Rd
Burke Road
Macaulay Rd
Kingsley Close
Shirley Close
Castle Hill J&I Sch
Palmcroft Cl
Palmcroft Road
Fircroft Road
Pearcroft Road
Arnold Close
Burke Cl
Bunyan Close
Congreve Road
Aldercroft Road
Aldercroft Close
Wrdswrth Crs
Swinburne Rd
Road
Burns Rd
Garrick Way
Castle Hill
Larchcroft Road
Birchcroft Rd
Larchcroft Close
Stratford
St Pancras RC Primary School
Cedarcroft
Charlton Av
Preston Drive
Pinecroft Road
Willowcroft Road
Elmcroft
Fircroft Road
Congreve Rd
Rosecroft Road
Hazelcroft Rd
Larchcroft Road
Clive Av
June Avenue
Meredith Rd
Surgery
Chesterfield Drive
Tranmere Grove
Beechcroft Road
IP1
Road
Dale
Dale Hall Primary School
White House
Highfield Road
M A
Chelsea Close
Everton Crescent
Ashcroft
Queensdale Close
Dales Road
Baronsdale Cl
Hall
Karen Close
The Grove
Vere Gdns
Shrubland Av
Ravensfield Road
NORWICH
Hghfl Ap
Works
Knightsdale Road
Wharfedale Road
Castle Road
Rayleigh Road
Lister Road
Kelvin Rd
Deben Rd
Westbourne Road
Cromer Rd
Westbourne High School
Westbourne
Princedale Cl
Dales Road
Silverdale Close
Cheltenham Avenue
Onehouse Lane
Lane
Ipswich Sports Club
ROAD
Mornington Avenue
Westholme Road
Dales View Road
Park Vw Rd
Pine Av
View Rd
Cotswold Avenue
Woodstone
Henley Road
Dale Hall Lane
Elsmere
VALLEY
Mumford Road
Waveney Road
Wallace Road
Broadmere Rd
Vincent Close
Eustace Rd
Pitcairn Road
Edward Cl
Kingston Road
Thompson Rd
Mt Rd
Brookfield Rd
Ch Cl
Springfield Lane
Kitchener Road
Springfield Junior Sch
Lwr Dales Vw Rd
Kensington Road
Sherrington Road
Broom Hill Swimming Pool
Broom Hl Rd
Westwood Av
Constitution
Brackenbury Close
Hill
Hotel
Greenways Close
St Edmund's Place
A1156
Quentin Cl
Road
Wesley Wy
Surbiton Road
Richmond Rd
Bramford
Lambeth Close
All Saints' Road
Brooks Hall Rd
Surg
Grh Av
Graham Road
St Edmund's Road
Paget Road
Brighton Road
Warrington Road
Holly Road
Ipswich School
Henley Road
Business Park
Boss Hall Rd
Hall
BRAMFORD ROAD
Riverside Rd
Hampton Road
Windsor Rd
S C
Waterloo Road
Providence Lane
CHEVALLIER ST
Gipping Va
Tanners View
Dhobi Place
Arkwright Road
River
Tower Ml Rd
Bramford La
Wellington St
NORW
Anglesea Rd
Ivry
Anglesea
Bowthorpe Cl
Oban St
Rdn St
Cardigan
Street
Surgery
Road
B11

12
Westerfield
Sparrowe's Nest
Lower Road
Sandy
Field Fuller's
Swan Lane
St Marys Way
Church
Westerfield Business Centre
LC
Westerfield Station
WESTERFIELD ROAD
Red House Farm
Tuddenham Road
Grove Farm
The Grove
Vere Gdns
Ipswich Sports Club
Valley Close
Bromeswell Road
Chelsworth Avenue
Dorset Cl
Picton Avenue
Valley Road
Colchester Rd
A1214
VALLEY ROAD
Woodstone Av
Kingsfield Avenue
Brettenham Crs
The Avenue
Borrowdale Av
North Close
Berkeley Cl
Belgrave Cl
Carlton Wy
Ipswich Crematorium
Cemetery Lane
New Cemetery
Old Cemetery
The Albany
South Close
Elsmere Rd
Hotel
Park Road
Manor Road
Corder Road
Gainsborough Rd
Constable
Henley Road
Dale Hall Lane
Hill
Greenways Close
St Edmund's Place
St Edmund's Road
Constitution
Ipswich School
Christchurch Park
Holly Road
Warrington Road
Broughton Road
Ivry Street
Surgery
IPSWICH
B1077
Vermont Road
Vermont Crescent
Bransby Gdns
Belvedere Road
Moat Farm Close
Brunswick Road
Somerset Road
Beverley Rd
Whitby Road
Parade Road
Stuart Cl
Lonsdale Cl
Hutland
Clare Road
Queens Drive
PO
Henley Road
Henley Rd
Drive
Lincoln Cl
Lincoln Close
Henley Avenue
Pearcroft Road
Aldercroft Close
Larchcroft Road
Larchcroft Close
Clive Av
Dale
Hall
Karen Close
Baronsdale Cl
Stonehouse Lane
Cotswold Avenue
Thurleston Lane
Woodwood Close
A B C D
1 2 3 4 5
11
22
616 17 48 47 246
1 grid square represents 500 metres

Westerfield Lane
Main Road
Green Lane
Valley Walk
Westerfield House
Humber Doucy Lane
Tuddenham Lane
Lamberts Lane
Hill Farm
Ipswich RUFC
Seven Cottages Lane
Inverness Road
Sherborne Avenue
Wincanton Cl
Cranborne Chase
Sidegate Lane
Angus Cl
Ayr Rd
Lanark Rd
Kinross Road
Renfrew Road
Moffat Av
Roxburgh Rd
Glencoe Road
Selkirk Rd
Dumbarton Road
Aberdeen Wy
Forfar Cl
Troon Gdns
Ross Rd
Fife Rd
Rnfrw Rd
Melrose Gdns
Cromarty Rd
Caithness Close
Rushmere Hall Primary School
Alma Close
Orkney Rd
Shetland Cl
Shetland Close
COLCHESTER ROAD A1214
Sidegate Av
Rushbury Close
Leopold Road
Leopold Gdns
Westbury Road
Glenhurst Avenue
Norbury Rd
North Lawn
West Lawn
The Lawns
East Lawn
Winston Avenue
Thornley Drive
Rushmere Road
Rushmere Street
The Limes
Birchwood Drive
Holly Lane
Chestnut Close
Rushmere Sports Club
Rushmere St Andrew
Summerfield Close
Playford Road
Playford Rd
The Mills
Sidegate Primary School
St Johns CE Primary School
IP4
Stradbroke Road
Bristol Rd
Victory Road
Rushmere Road
Schreiber Road
Digby Road
Mayfield Road
Mayfield Rd
Ladywood Road
Lindsey Road
St Albans Catholic High School
WOODBRIDGE RD EAST A1214 WOODBRIDGE
Cherry Gdns
PO
19
20
48
47
246
E
F
G
H
I
2
3
4
5
14
23

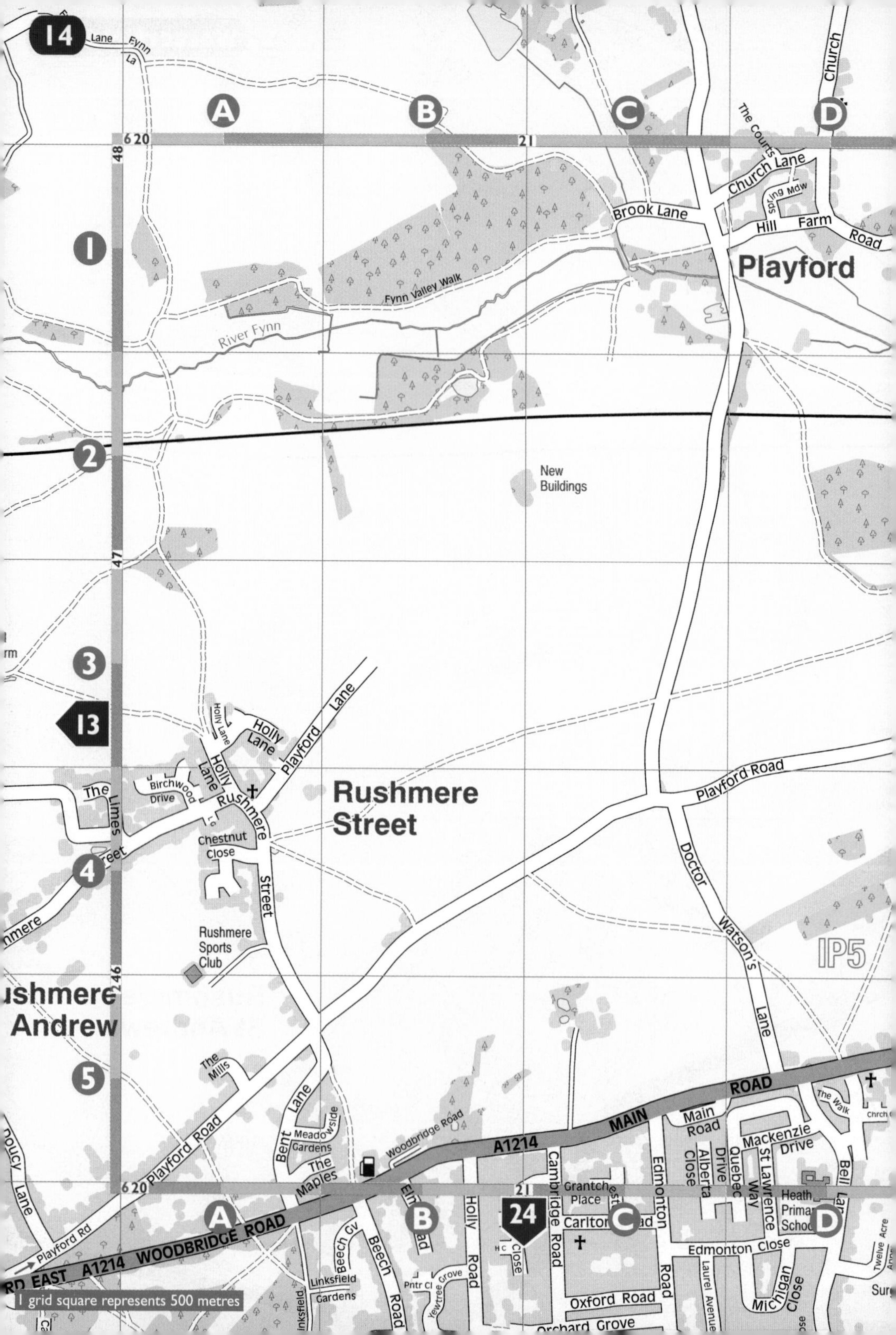

14
13
24
Playford
Rushmere Street
Rushmere St Andrew
New Buildings
Brook Lane
Church Lane
Hill Farm Road
Spring Mdw
The Courts
Church
Fynn Valley Walk
River Fynn
Fynn Lane
Holly Lane
Playford Lane
Birchwood Drive
The Limes
Chestnut Close
Rushmere Street
Rushmere Sports Club
Playford Road
Doctor Watson's Lane
IP5
The Mills
Bent Lane
Meadowside Gardens
The Maples
Woodbridge Road
A1214 MAIN ROAD
A1214 WOODBRIDGE ROAD
Main Road
Cambridge Road
Grantchester Place
Carlton Road
Edmonton Road
Edmonton Close
Alberta Close
Quebec Drive
St Lawrence Way
Mackenzie Drive
The Walk
Bell Lane
Heath Primary School
Holly Road
Beech Road
Beech Gv
Linksfield Gardens
Yewtree Grove
Pntr Cl
Oxford Road
Orchard Grove
Laurel Avenue
Michigan Close
Twelve Acre
Doucy Lane
Playford Rd
1 grid square represents 500 metres

Little Bealings
Beacon Hill
Kesgrave Hall
Kesgrave County High School
Gorseland Primary Scho
Mallard House Business Cen
Bealings School
The Grove
Lux Farm
River Fynn
Fynn Valley Walk
Holly Close
Lane
Lodge Road
Michaels Mount
Richards Drive
Sandy Lane
The Street
LC
Beacon Lane
Martlesham Road
Playford Road
Hall Road
A12
A1214
MAIN ROAD
Portal Avenue
Peel Yard
Bracken Avenue
Dobbs Lane
Deben Avenue
Stephen Road
Gayfer Avenue
Grange Close
Grange Lane
Dobbs Lane
Copswood Close
Dobbs Drift
St Olaves Road
Windrush Road
Emerald Close
Ashdale Road
Wright Lane
Wainwright Way
Ropes Drive
The Whinneys
Howards Way
Booth Lane
Through Jollys
Friends Walk
Herbert Road
Fletchers Lane
Largent Grove
Gostling Place
Francis Close
Fox Lea
Mannall Walk
Page Gardens
Fentons Way
Cardew Drift
Arkle Court
The Bretts
Cooks Cl
Turner Gv
Stmmrs Pl
Reeve Gardens
Scopes Rd
Jewell Vw
Fentons Way
Dewar Lane
Cranwell Grove
Crawford Lane
Fairbairn Avenue
Knights Lane
Elmers Lane
Deben Valley Drive
Dodson Vale
Sheppards Way
Wilding Drive
Batties Lane
Ropes Drive
Bugsby Way
Haskins Walk
Peacock St
Jeavons Lane
Broomfield
Broomfield Mews
Whinfield
Eagle Close
Carlford Close
Saddlers Place
Valiant Road
Eagle
The Grove
Martl
PO
E
F
G
H
I
2
3
4
5
16
25
23
24
48
47
246

1 grid square represents 500 metres

Maidensgrave
Briarwood Rd
Sandy Lane
E
F
9
G
H
27
28
48
Broom Hill
Broomheath
Fynn Va Wk
I
Haddon Hall
Kingston
2
47
3
4
Waldringfield Road
Woodbridge Road
246
5
Moon & Sixpence
Waldringfield Rd

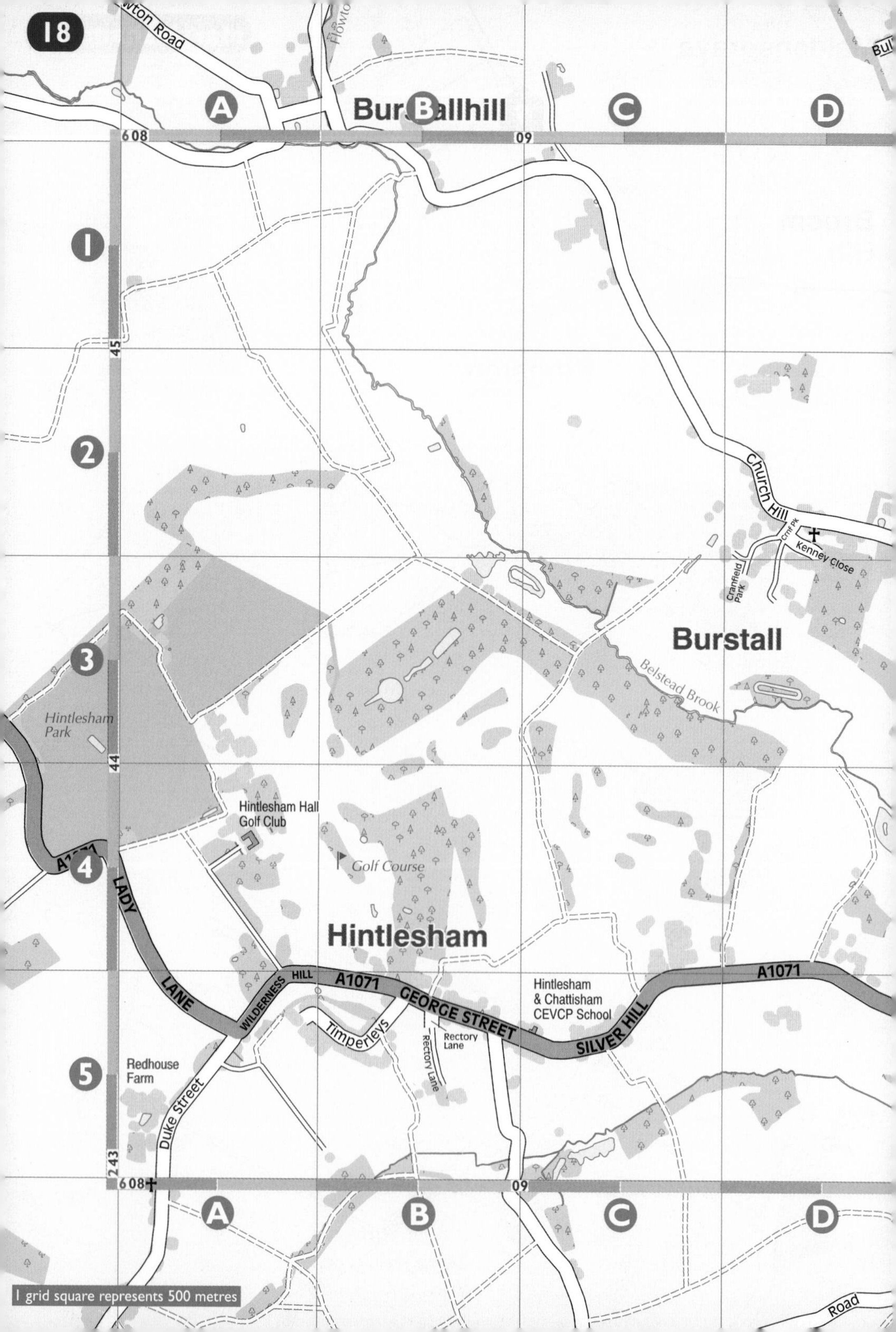
Burstallhill
Burstall
Hintlesham
Hintlesham Park
Hintlesham Hall Golf Club
Golf Course
Belstead Brook
Church Hill
Kenney Close
Cranfield Park
Crnf Pk
Lady Lane
Wilderness Hill
A1071
George Street
Silver Hill
Timperleys
Rectory Lane
Duke Street
Hintlesham & Chattisham CEVCP School
Redhouse Farm
Flowton Road
Road
A
B
C
D
1
2
3
4
5
608
09
45
44
243
1 grid square represents 500 metres

E
F
G
H
11
12
Grindle Farm
The Grindle
B1113
1
45
Burstall Lane
Ransome Close
HIGH STREET
2
Abbey Oaks
Burstall Lane
PO
3
20
44
Ivywell Farm
HURDLE MAKERS HILL
A1071
A1071
4
Burstall Bridge
Fen Farm
THORPE'S HILL
Valley Farm
5
Belstead Brook
Pigeon's Lane
243
Lower Barn Road
E
F
28
G
H
The Grange
Washbrook Street
Spring

20
10
19
29
Runcton Farm
Sproughton Manor
Grindle Farm
The Grindle
B1113
River Gipping
Sproughton Business Park
Farthing Road Industrial Estate
Farthing Road
Sproughton Road
Sproughton Rd
Lower St
Sproughton
Burstall Lane
HIGH STREET
Beech Close
Church Crs
Church Lane
Glebe Cl
Ransome Close
Oak Gv
Samford Place
Broomfield Common
Gipping Wy
Sproughton CE Primary School
Monks Gate
Gipping Valley River Path
A14(T)
Nine Acres
Daundy Cl
Barker Close
Collinson's
Ventris Close
Church Lane
Larchwood Cl
Orchard Gate
Red House
Hadleigh Road
Chantry Park
Springvale
A1071
Poplar Farm
Poplar Lane
Hotel
LONDON ROAD
A1214
London Rd
Swallow Rd
Robin Dr
Wren Av
Curlew Road
Teal Close
Works
Sprites La
Merlin Rd
Greenfinch Avenue
Goldcrest Road
Stonechat Rd
Kestrel Rd
Woodpecker Rd
Bunting Rd
Chantry Green
Chantry Close
Scrivener Dr
Shepherd Dr
Sprites Junior School
Surg
Hawthorn
Denton Cl
Didsbury Cl
Hale Cl
Bridgwater
The Chestnuts
Milnrow
Ashton Cl
Wentworth Dr
Halford Ct
Chamberlain Wy
Pigeon's Lane
Europa Way
Spinner Close
Lone Barn Ct
Weaver Cl
SAMFORD ROAD
Whitworth Close
Middleton Close
1 grid square represents 500 metres

Broom Hill Swimming Pool
Springfield Junior Sch
Springfield Lane
Kitchener Road
Sherrington Road
Westwood Av
Constitution
St Edmund's Road
Graham Road
Bramford Road
Bramford La
All Saints' Road
Brooks Hall Rd
Chevallier St
Norwich Road
Anglesea Rd
Ivry Street
Surgery
Warrington Road
Henley Road
Ipswich School
Boss Hall Rd
Business Park
Gipping Va
River Gipping
Crompton Road
Hadleigh Road Ind Est
Arkwright Road
Whittle Road
Brunel Rd
Brookhouse Business Park
Superstore
Hadleigh Road
Handford Hall Primary Sch
Suffolk Retail Park
Sikh Temple
Service Centre
Yarmouth Rd
London Road
Handford Road A1071
Berners Street
Nuffield Hospital
Ipswich Mus & Art Gal
BBC Radio
Wolsey Thtr
Crown Ct
Civic Dr
St Mathew's St
Mkt
Civ Cen
Town Hall
Co Court
Pol Stn
Mag Ct
Princes St
Willis Corroon Building
Orwell Retail Park
Ranelagh Primary Sch
Portmans Wk Industrial Cen
Sir Alf Ramsey Way
Ipswich Town FC (Portman Road)
Bus Depot
West End Rd
Portman Rd
Russell Road
Fire Stn
Quadling St
RM Sorting Off
Commercial Rd
Grafton Way
Friars
Retail Park
Works
Ranelagh Road B1075
Gipping Park
Gippeswyk Park
Burrell Road B1073
Ipswich Station
Gippeswyk Avenue
Grantham Crs
Belstead Road
Stoke
Philip Rd
Luther Road
Rectory Road
Belstead Av
A1214
Lavenham Rd
Dickens Road
Business Cen
Waller's Grove
Speedwell Road
Lavender Hill
Campion Rd
Birkfield Close
Birkfield Drive
Chantry J&I School
Shamrock Av
Marigold Av
Hawthorn Drive
Hawthorn Dr
St Marks RC Primary Sch
Stone Lodge Lane West
Stone Lodge Walk
Beacon Hill Special School
Chantry
Chantry High School
IP2
St Josephs Prep School & College
Heatherhayes
Pembroke Close
Maidenhall Approach
Hillside Community Primary Sch
Stoke County High School
Halifax Primary Sch
Prince of Wales Drive
Maidenhall Sports Centre
Sheldrake Drive
Mallard Way
Plover Road
Kirkham Close
Byland Close
Fernhayes Cl
Conway Cl
E F G H I
11 22 30 2 3 4 5
15 16

22
IPSWICH
Stoke
Park Road
Constitution Hill
St Edmund's Road
Westerfield Road
Manor Road
Corder Road
Gainsborough Rd
Whitby Road
Beverley Rd
Somerset Road
New Cemetery
Cemetery
Christchurch Park
Christchurch Mansion
Ipswich School
Henley Road
Nuffield Hospital
Fonnereau Rd
Ipswich Mus & Art Gal
Crown St
St Mathew's St
Crown Pools
Charles St
Claude St
Bolton La
B1077
St Margarets CE Primary School
Tuddenham Road
Vermont Crescent
Suffolk Road
Cemetery Road
Woodbridge Rd
A1071
Albion Hl
St Marys Catholic Primary School
Spring Road
Alexandra Road
Belle Vue Road
Haslemere Drive
Bank Road
Lacey Street
St Helens Primary Sch
St Helens St
St Helen's Street
Grimwade St
Bond St
Rope Wk
Council Building
Suffolk College
Alexandra Park
Grove Lane
B1075
Clifford Road Primary School
Woodville Rd
Back Hamlet
Fore St
Fore Hamlet
Bishop's Hill
Duke St B1458
Cliff Road
Holy Wells Rd
Holywells Park
Wet Dock
Patteson Road
Neptune Quay
Old Customs House
Key St
College St
Star La
Grafton Way
Commercial Rd
B1075
Princes St
Friars Rd
Civic Dr
Portman Rd
Willis Corroon Building
Cardinal Park
UGC
Buttermkt Shop Cen
Ancient Ho
Town Hall
Corn Exchange
Customs & Excise
Almshouses
Blackfriars Priory Hall
Salvation Army
Eastgate Shop Cen
Odeon
Stoke Bridge
Bridge St
Vernon St
Burrell Road B1073
Retail Park
Ipswich Station
Belstead Road
Luther Road
Philip Rd
Rectory Road
Station St
Croft St
Wherstead Road
Hawes St
Felaw St
Stoke Quay
Purplett Street
Bath St
Riverside Ind Park
Hillside Community Primary Sch
Stoke County High School
Johnson Close
Cowell Street
Maidenhall Approach
Maidenhall Sports Centre
Brecon Close
Brewery Museum
Greenwich Business Park
Orwell Business Centre
Greenwich Road
Cliff Lane Primary School
Dereham Avenue
Oulton Rd
Medway Road
Suffolk Coast & Heaths Pth
River Orwell
Works
1 grid square represents 500 metres
A B C D
1 2 3 4 5
12
21
31
3

Colchester Road
A1214
Sidegate Av
Caithness Close
Rushbury Close
Westbury Road
Glenhurst
Leopold Road
Leopold Gdns
Norbury Rd
North Lawn
The Lawns
East Lawn
Winston Avenue
Thornley Drive
Humber Doucy Lane
Summerfield Close
Rushmere Road
13
Sidegate Primary School
St Johns CE Primary School
IP4
Mayfield Road
Fawley Close
Ladywood Road
Digby Road
St Albans Catholic High School
Playford Road
Playford Rd
Woodbridge Rd East
A1214 Woodbridge
Roundwood Road
Victory Road
Stradbroke Road
Bristol Rd
Phoenix Road
Schreiber Road
Reading Rd
Jupiter Road
Cherry La
Gdns
Crofton Road
Lindsey Road
PO
Glenavon Rd
Camberley Rd
Melbourne Rd
A1071 Woodbridge Road
Gordon Road
Kirby Close
Kirby Street
Milton St
Howard St
Millfield Gdns
Kennedy Close
The Drift
Cauldwell Hall Road
Spring Road
Springland
Upland Rd
Ringham Road
Tolworth Rd
Mandy Close
Crabbe Street
Cowper Street
Sunfield Close
Bloomfield St
Starfield Close
Ernleigh Road
Halliwell Road
Britannia Road
Thanet Road
The Driftway
SC
Risby Cl
Goring Road
Lattice Avenue
Surgery
Ipswich Hospital
A&E
A1189
Heath Road
Adelaide Rd
Rushmere Golf Club
Tasmania Road
Brisbane Rd
CCl
Golf Course
Rushmere Heath
California
Freehold Road
Newbury Road
Heathside Special School
Copleston High School
Copleston Road
Regina Close
St Aubyns Rd
Hillary Cl
Geralds Av
Derby Close
Kembal Street
Churchill Avenue
Harrow Cl
Chrt Cl
W Cl
Henslow Road
Randwell Close
Parliament Road
Brittania Primary School
Lyndhurst Av
Heath Lane
Gleneagles Drive
Fairways
Works
Fuchsia Lane
E Rd
Churchill Av
Coronation Road
Roy Avenue
Walker Close
Pearson Road
SA Cl
Broke Hall Primary School
24
Tomline Rd
Foxhall Road
Derby Rd
Pearce Rd
Stanley Av
Orwell Road
Camden Road
Dover Road
Sunningdale Avenue
Civrtn Wy
Hardwick Close
Chatsworth
Overton Way
Civr Wy
York Rd
Derby Road Station
Rose Hill Primary School
Surg
St Clements Hospital
Chilton Road
Temple Road
Princethorpe Road
Penshurst Rd
Broke Hall Gdns
Wimborne Avenue
Derby Road
Exeter Road
CG
Hines Rd
Bixley Road
St Augustine Rd
Rye Close
Winfrith Road
Bodiam Rd
BC
MCl
Melplash Road
Arundel Way
Felixstowe Road
Osbr Rd
Levington Rd
Hatfield Road
Murray Road
King Edward Road
Malvern Close
Ascot Drive
Ramsgate Dr
RC
Bridport Av
Wareham Av
Cuckfield Avenue
St Augustine's Garden
Broke Hall
Blandford Road
Poole Close
Lulworth Av
Horsham Avenue
Salehurst Road
Clapgate Lane
Nacton Road
Hamilton Road
Pretyman Road
Locarno Road
Margate Rd
Dorchester Road
Wadhurst Road
Lewes Close
Beatrice Close
Badshah Av
Hillside Crs
Ftzmrc Rd
St Leonards Road
Shackleton Road
Sturdee Av
Howe Av
Drake Square North
Heather Av
Ashdown Way
Wye Rd
Murrayfield Primary School
St David's Rd
Ransome Crs
Ransome Rd
Drake Av
Franklin Rd
Bantoft Terrace
Cobham Rd
Bucklesham Road
Felixstowe
E
F
G
H
I
2
3
4
5
19
20
45
44
243
32
Rydal Walk
Wright Road
Ipswich Transport Museum
Queen's Way
Queen's Sq
Recn Wy
Packard Av
Coniston Road
Nansen Road
Nacton Crs
Henstead Gdns
Norman Crs
Benacre Road
Spriine Rd
Warren Heath Rd
Warren Heath Av
course

The Mills
Playford Road
Bent Lane
Meadowside
Meadow Gardens
The Maples
Woodbridge Road
MAIN ROAD
14
Main Road
The Walk
Chrch
Mackenzie Drive
Alberta Close
Quebec Drive
St Lawrence Way
Bell Lane
Heath Primary School
Twelve Acre
Surg
Cambridge Road
Grantchester Place
Carlton Road
Edmonton Road
Edmonton Close
Laurel Avenue
Michigan Close
Oxford Road
Orchard Grove
Montana Road
Roy Close
Oregon Road
Felix Close
Columbia Close
Cedar Avenue
Helston Close
Camborne Road
Penzance Road
St Ives Close
Falmouth Close
Bodmin Close
Padstow Road
Heath View
Glanville Place
Trinity Close
Holly Road
Elm Road
Beech Road
Beech Gv
Linksfield Gardens
Linksfield
Yewtree Grove
Pntr Cl
Mndp Cl
Quantock Close
St Agnes Wy
Penryn Road
St Austell Close
Mendip Drive
Blackdown Avenue
Barnham Place
Flibrgg Av
Brendon Drive
Ditchingham Grove
M Crs
Finborough Close
Hg Dr
Giffords Place
Euston Avenue
Broadlands Way
Seckford Close
Parnham Place
M Cl
Foxhall Heath Stadium
Sandling Crescent
Butterfly Gdns
Larkhill Rl
Shrubland Drive
The Fairways
S Pl
Foxwood Crescent
F Pl
Ickworth Crescent
Kelvedon Drive
Pardoe Place
Bixley Drive
Blair Close
Sandpit Close
Bixley Lane
Bladen Drive
Broadlands Way
The Pastures
Hghtn Pl
Newby Dr
Melford Close
Glemham Drive
Kentwell Close
Gwendoline Road
Clovelly Close
Foxhall Road
Brookhill Wood
Surgery
Mere Gardens
The Greens
Western Close
E C
Brookhill Way
The Spinney
Valleyview Drive
Brook Hill
Heathlands Park
A1214 WOODBRIDGE ROAD
RD EAST
Playford Rd
Camberley Rd
Rushmere Golf Club
Golf Course
Rushmere Heath
Tasmania Road
Golf Course
Gleneagles Drive
S A Cl
Broke Hall Primary School
23
Sunningdale Avenue
Clvrtn W
Hardwick Close
Chatsworth Dr
Claverton Way
Clvr Wy
Broke Hall Gdns
Foxhall Road
Wimborne Avenue
Rye Close
M Cl
Bodiam Rd
Melplash Road
Arundel Way
Winfrith Road
Wareham Av
Surgery
Cuckfield Avenue
Lulworth Way
Horsham Avenue
Salehurst Road
Wadhurst Road
Dorchester Road
Lewes Close
Golf Course
Ipswich Golf Club
33
Purdis Farm
Purdis
Farm Lane
Road
620
21
45
44
243
A
B
C
D
1
2
3
4
5
1 grid square represents 500 metres

15
23
24
E
F
G
H
I
2
3
4
5
26
34
45
44
243
Emerald Close
Windrush Road
Ashdale Road
St Olaves Road
Wright Lane
Wainwright Way
Turner Gv
Ropes
Through Jollys
Friends Walk
Howards Way
Booth Lane
Herbert Road
Largent Grove
Gostling Place
Mannall Walk
Francis Close
Fox Lea
Page Gardens
Stephen Road
Grange Close
Grange Lane
Gayfer Avenue
Dobbs Lane
Kers Place
The Grove
Eagle Close
Carlford Close
Whinfield
Broomfield
Broomfield Mews
Saddlers Place
Valiant
Westland
Eagle Way
Gorseland Primary School
Copswood Close
Dobbs Drift
Fentons Way
Fentons Way
Cardew Drift
Saint Isidores
Bugsby Way
Haskins Walk
Fairbairn Avenue
Dewar Lane
Cranwell Grove
Wolton Road
Crawford Lane
Knights Lane
Elmers Lane
Battles Lane
Wilding Drive
Sheppards Way
Deben Valley Drive
Dodson Vale
Lummis Vale
Rowarth Avenue
The Lloyds
Ropes Drive
Peacock St
Jeavons Lane
Howlett Cl
Bailey Av
Century Dr
Masterson Gv
Adams Place
Harvester Way
Lingside
Forest Lane
Pine Bank
The Oaks
Holly End
Heathfield
Heathfield Mews
Heather Close
Digby Close
Mayfields Lane
Eagle Way
Dobbs Lane
Foxhall Heath
Pole Hill
Foxhall Road
Foxhall Road
Hall Road
Foxhall Hall
Monument Farm Road
Mill River
Springbank Industrial Estate
Hall Road
Valley Farm
A12(T)
Kennels Road
Monument Farm
Lodge Farm
Kennels Road
Purdis Farm Lane
Purdis Road
Wood House

Martlesham Heath
Brightwell
A12
A12(T)
Eagle Way
Valiant Road
The Drift
Surgery
Birchwood County Primary Sch
Westland
Broomfield
Broomfield Mews
Warren Lane
Swan Close
Lark Rise
Coopers Road
Avocet Lane
Forest Lane
Lingside
Harvest Way
Oaks
Birch Grove
York Road
Lancaster Drive
Mayfield Lane
Mayfields
Digby Close
Heathfield
Heathfield Mews
Heather Close
Carlford Close
Saddlers Place
Farriers Close
The Chase
Manor Road
Beardmore Park
Martinsyde
Gloster Road
Hawker Dr
Hilton Road
Betts Avenue
Works
Barrack Square
Milano Ave
St Gotthards Ave
Geneva Ave
Lugano Ave
Roma Ave
Turino Ave
Heath Road
Newbourne Road
Newbourne
Foxhall Road
Kennels Road
PO
16
25
35
1 grid square represents 500 metres

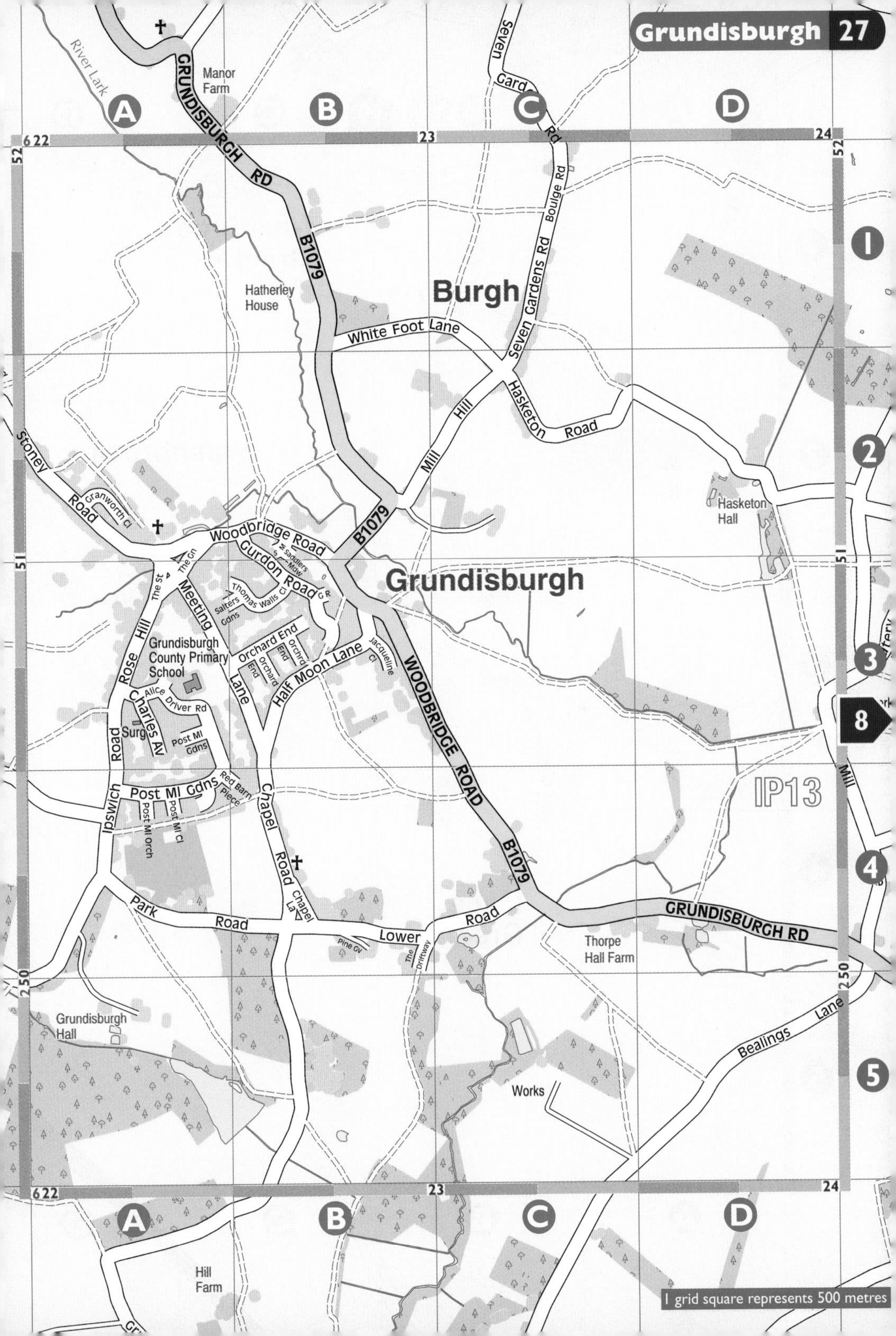

1 grid square represents 500 metres

19
A
B
C
D
1
2
3
4
5
610
11
43
42
241
Valley Farm
Belstead Brook
Pigeon's Lane
The Grange
Washbrook Street
Lower Barn Road
Road
Spring Road
Wood's Hill
Amor Hall
Washbrook
Church Lane
Fen Farm
Street
Charlotte's
Pearsons
Pheasant Rl
Back Lane
Copdock Primary School
The
School Hill
Fen Vw
Dales Vw
Fen Vw
London Road
Hollow Road
Coles Green
Saxon Lane
Elm Lane
Wenham Road
Copdock
Copdock Cricket Club
Mace Green
Hotel
The Avenue
The Grange Farm
A12(T)

Poplar Farm
Poplar Lane
Hotel
20
London Road
A1214
Works
Goldcrest Road
Stonechat Rd
Swallow Rd
Robin Dr
Greenfinch Avenue
Merlin Rd
Kestrel Rd
Bunting Rd
Redwing Cl
Chantry Clnc
Royston Dr
Sheldrake
Gannet Road
Hawthorn Drive
Scrivener Dr
Sprites La
Sprites Junior School
Shepherd Dr
Scrivener Drive
Surg
Whitworth Close
Middleton Close
Denton Cl
Didsbury Cl
Worsley Close
Manchester Rd
Dunlin Road
Sheldrake Dr
Chamberlain Wy
Wentworth Dr
Halford Ct
Skylark La
Milnrow
Ashton Cl
The Chestnuts
Radcliffe Dr
Holcombe Crs
Bridgwater Road
Hale Cl
Monton Ri
Atherton Rd
Wilmslow Drive
Shotley Cl
Acorn Cl
Ward Rd
Belstead School
Sprites Lane
Fir Tree Rise
Buttercup Cl
Acer Grove
Pin Ml Cl
Eccles Road
Woolverstone Cl
Pendleton Rd
Irlam Rd
Annbrook Rd
Tinabrook Cl
Oldfield Rd
Wilson Rd
Superstore
Superstore
London Road
Whights' Corner
A14(T)
Yewtree Ri
Belmont Rd
Sycamore Cl
Rudlands
Appleby Close
Bramhall Cl
Ellenbrook Road
Gusford Primary School
Wilding Road
Devlin Rd
Wilding Rd
Cottingham Road
Bowland Dr
Baldry Close
Knutsford Close
Quilter Drive
Shortlands
Wardley Close
Swinton Close
Dashwood Close
Grove Hill
Skipper Cl
Brimstone Rd
Ellenbrook Rd
Green Oak Glade
Burnet Close
Forest Cl
30
Holly Lane
Grove Hill
A14(T)
A12(T)
Lane
Belstead Hall
Chapel Lane
Belstead
Church La
Grove Hill
Road
Buck's Horns Lane
Thoring Hall
Blacksmith's Corner
The Street
Bentley Lane
E
F
G
H
I
2
3
4
5
13
14
43
42
241

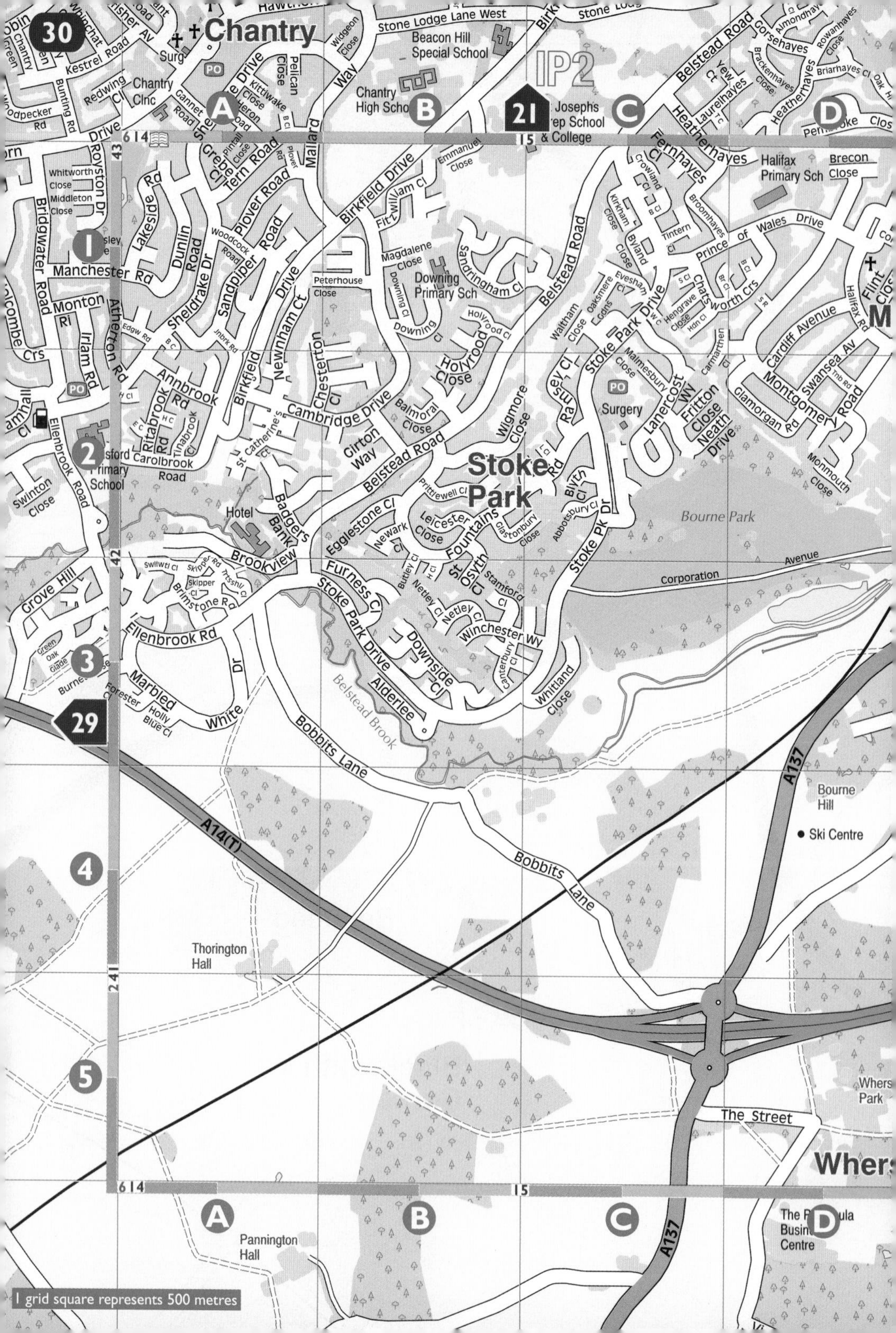

30
Chantry
Stone Lodge Lane West
Beacon Hill Special School
IP2
Chantry High School
21
St Josephs Prep School & College
Belstead Road
Halifax Primary Sch
Prince of Wales Drive
Manchester Rd
Atherton Rd
Bridgwater Road
Sheldrake Dr
Birkfield Drive
Downing Primary Sch
Sandringham Cl
Stoke Park Drive
Cambridge Drive
Belstead Road
Stoke Park
Surgery
Cardiff Avenue
Montgomery Road
Bourne Park
Corporation Avenue
Brookview
Ellenbrook Rd
Ellenbrook Road
Grove Hill
Stoke Park Drive
Belstead Brook
Bobbits Lane
29
A14(T)
A137
Bourne Hill
Ski Centre
Thorington Hall
The Street
Whers Park
Pannington Hall
The Peninsula Business Centre
1 grid square represents 500 metres

Riverside Ind Park
Brewery Museum
Cliff Lane Primary School
Greenwich Business Park
Orwell Business Centre
Greenwich Road
Landseer Road
Landseer Park
Racecourse
River Orwell
Cliff Quay
Greenwich
A137 WHERSTEAD ROAD
Works
Orwell Yacht Club
Hawke Road
Robeck Road
Sandyhill Lane
Orwell Junior School
Raeburn Infant School
Raeburn Road
Raeburn Road South
Hogarth Road
Fletcher Road
Romney Road
Reynolds Rd
Turner Road
Gainsborough Lane
Orwell Country Park
Pipers Vale
New Channel
THE STRAND
B1456
A14(T)
Orwell Bridge
Pond Hall Farm
Suffolk Coast & Heaths Pth
Morland Prim School
Severn Road
Derwent Road
Trent Road
Medway Road
Dereham Avenue
Mersey Road
Wroxham Road
Oulton Rd
Wye Rd
22
32

32
23
31
Broke Hall
Racecourse
Priory Heath
Gainsborough
IP3
Murrayfield Primary School
Works
Ipswich Transport Museum
Holywells High School
Raeburn Infant School
Morland Primary School
Gainsborough Sports Centre
Ind Park
Euro Park
Ransomes Industrial Park
Ipswich Airport (disused)
Pond Hall Farm
Orwell Bridge
Priory Park
Bridge Wood
Alnesbourne Priory Golf Club
Nacton Road
Felixstowe Road
A14(T)
A1189
Suffolk Coast & Heaths Path
1 grid square represents 500 metres

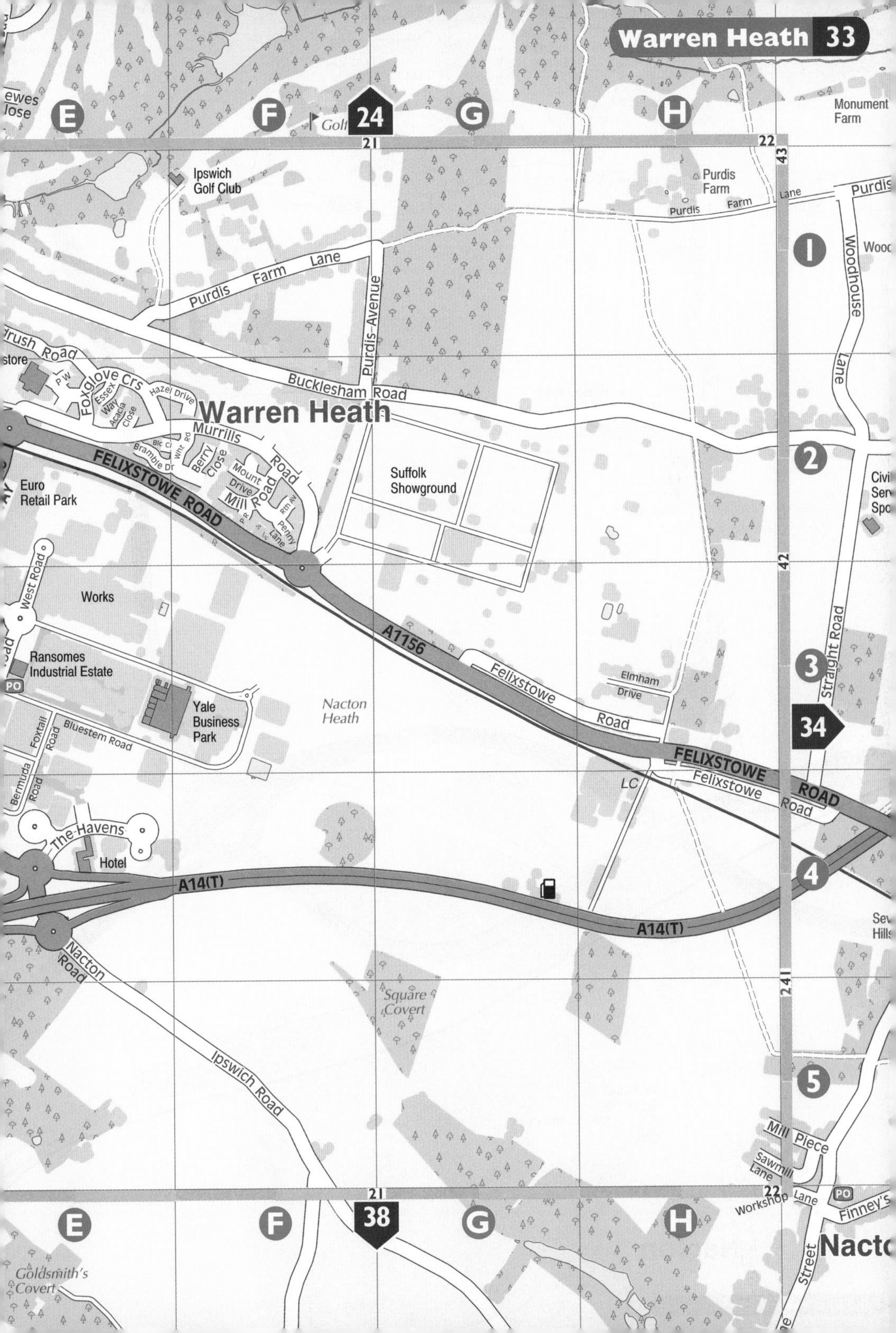
E
F
G
H
24
21
22
Golf
Monument Farm
Ipswich Golf Club
Purdis Farm
Purdis Farm Lane
Purdis
Purdis Farm Lane
Purdis Avenue
Woodhouse Lane
I
Bucklesham Road
Warren Heath
Foxglove Crs
Hazel Drive
Essex Way
Acacia Close
Murrills Road
Berry Close
Brambie Dr
Mount Drive
Mill Road
Penny Lane
FELIXSTOWE ROAD
Euro Retail Park
Suffolk Showground
2
43
42
Works
West Road
Ransomes Industrial Estate
PO
Yale Business Park
Bluestem Road
Foxtail Road
Bermuda Road
Nacton Heath
A1156
Felixstowe Road
Elmham Drive
3
Straight Road
34
FELIXSTOWE ROAD
Felixstowe Road
LC
The Havens
Hotel
A14(T)
A14(T)
4
Nacton Road
Square Covert
Ipswich Road
241
5
Mill Piece
Sawmill Lane
Workshop Lane
PO
Finney's
38
Goldsmith's Covert
Street
Nacto

Springbank
Industrial
Estate
Road
Hall Road
Valley
Farm
Monu
Farm
A
B
25
C
D
6 22
23
Lodge Farm
Road
43
Purdis
Farm
Purdis Farm Lane
Purdis Farm Lane
Purdis
Road
Kennels
1
Wood House
Woodhouse
Lane
Low House Touring
Caravan Centre
Bucklesham Road
2
Civil
Service
Sports Club
A12(T)
42
Straight Road
3
33
A14(T)
FELIXSTOWE
ROAD
Felixstowe
Road
4
A1156
A14(T)
(T)
Seven
Hills
241
Felixstowe
Road
5
Amberfield
School
Amberfield
Mill Piece
Sawmill
Lane
6 22
PO
Finney's Drift
Workshop Lane
23
A
B
39
C
D
Nacton
Street
1 grid square represents 500 metres

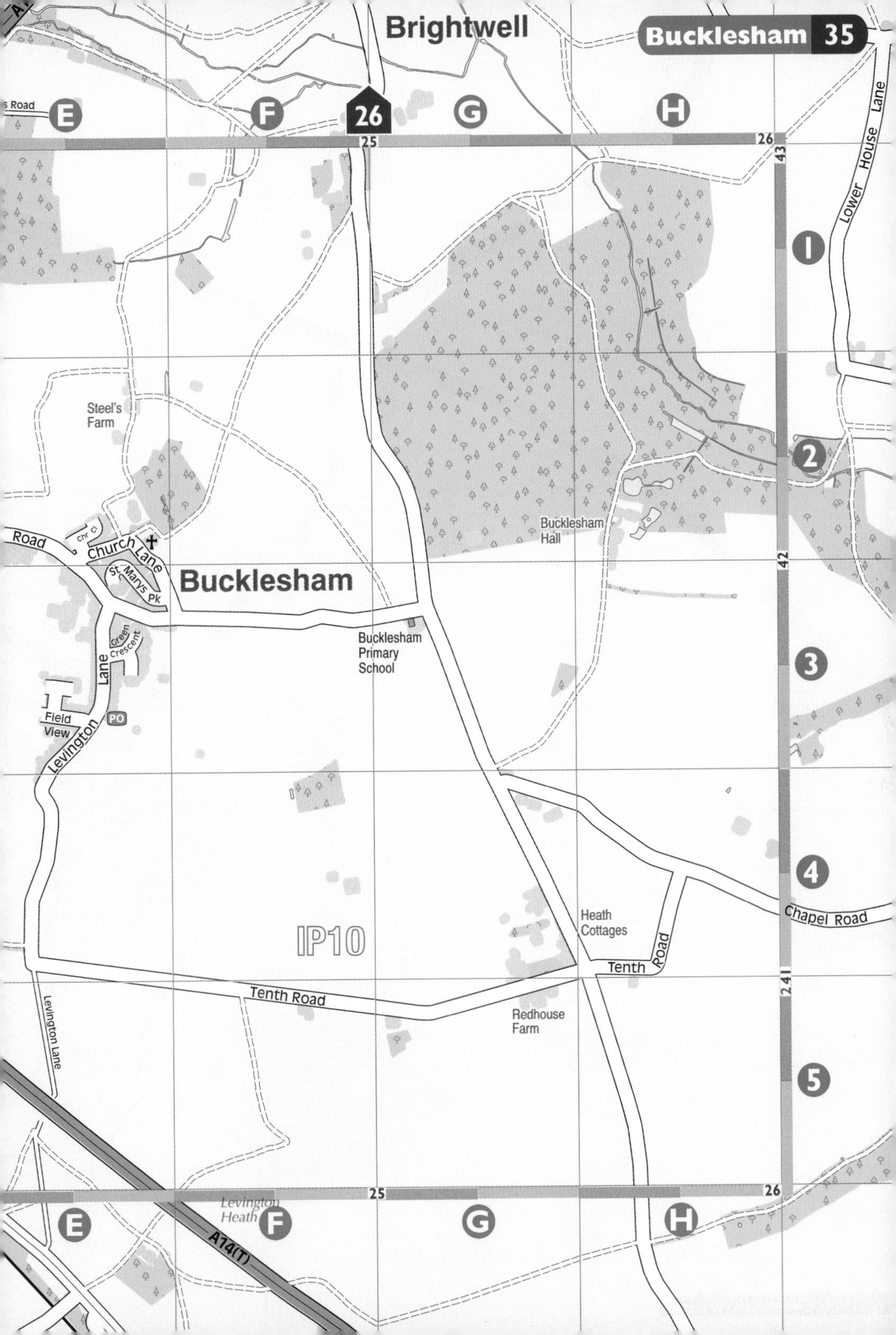
Brightwell
26
E
F
G
H
25
26
43
42
41
I
2
3
4
5
Lower House Lane
Steel's Farm
Road
Chr Cl
Church Lane
St Marys Pk
Bucklesham
Bucklesham Hall
Green Crescent
Bucklesham Primary School
Field View
PO
Levington Lane
IP10
Chapel Road
Heath Cottages
Tenth Road
Redhouse Farm
Levington Heath
A14(T)

Mill Lane
A
B
C
D
601
02
44
Noaks Tye Farm
A1141
River Brett
STONE STREET
Mill Hill
Aldham
Peyton Hall
1
A1071
Aldham Mill Hill
B1070
Gallows Hl
Castle Rd
Castle Rd
Castle Road
Castle Rl
GALLOWS HL
IP7
River Brett
2
Castle La
Ann Beaumont Wy
Ann Beaumont Wy
Ann Beaumont Wy
Sun Court
Boswell
Freeman Cl
Bradfield
Woodlands
43
Friars Rd
Council Building
BRIDGE ST
Calais St
Pykenham Wy
Pykenham Way
Meadows Wy
Mdws Wy
Coram Street
Coram Street
Corks Lane
Spooners Cl
ANGEL ST
3
Friars Hall Farm
HIGH STREET
Inkerman Cl
Inkerman Ter
Brett Works
Pound La
Magdalen Road
Cncl Bldg
Constitutional Hill
Church St
PO
Guthrum Rd
Fozel Thtr
The Guildhall
Corn Exchange
Market Pl
Health Cen
4
Silk Mill Cl
Duke St
B1070
Toppesfield Cl
Lane
Park Farm
Holbecks
242
Tinker's La
Layham Rd
Hadleigh RUFC
5
Holbecks
601
02
Pott's Farm
A
B
C
D
Hill Farm
1 grid square represents 500 metres

E
F
G
H
04
05
44
43
42
1
2
3
4
5
Wolves Wood (Nature Reserve)
A1071
Red Hill Road
Hill
Lane
Farm
Wolves Farm
Wolves
A1071 IPSWICH ROAD
IPSWICH ROAD
Cobbold Farm
Lady Lane Industrial Estate
LADY LANE
Ramsey Road
Ramsey Rd
Brett Av
Delf Cl
Nwhvn Wy
Timperley Road
Hadleigh
A1070
New Cut
The Gn
Tower Mill La
Canterbury Gdns
Cnt Gdn
Fullers Cl
Drapers Cl
St Marys Primary School
Edwin
Brnes Cl
Panks Road
Frog Hall Lane
Frog Hall
Valley Farm
Bourchier Cl
Pool
Tylr Rd
Yeoman Way
Rousies Cl
Sch Cl
Jordayn Cl
French's Farm
Hadleigh High School
Road
Wilson Rd
Banks Cl
Dunn Cl
Woodthorpe Road
Cottesford Cl
Lister Rd
Shearman Rd
Wdthpe Cl
Dyer Ct
Wentworth Cl
Buckenham Rd
Mrtn Rl
Aylward Cl
Glanville Road
Carlton Wk
Stockton Cl
Clopton Gdns
Cranworth Rd
Valley Farm Lane
Works
Pond Hall Road
Pond Hall Rd
Pond Hall Farm
Hadleigh Business Park
Works
Hook Lane
Town House Fruit Farm
STREET
Hadleigh Railway Walk
Kate's Hill Farm

38
33
A
B
C
D
620
21
Ipswich Road
Goldsmith's Covert
Park Farm
Ipswich
Road
Ipswich Rd
Church Road
Orwell Park School
Orwell Park House
40
39
238
1
2
3
4
5
Hall Point
River
Suffolk Coast & Heaths Path
Pin Mill
PH
Suffolk Coast Heaths Path
Orwell Rise
Pinmill
1 grid square represents 500 metres

Road
Amberfield School
Amberfield
E
F
34
G
H
23
24
PO
Finney's Drift
Nacton
I
Bridge Road
CE
ary School
40
2
Levington Road
Red House Walk
Bridge Road
Suffolk Coast & Heaths Path
3
Levington
Broke Hall
Church
PH
Lane
39
Suffolk Coast & Heaths Path
Strattonhall Drift
4
Orwell
5
238
23
24
E
F
G
H

Little Wenham
Jermyns Farm
Gipsy Row
Brook Lane
Days Road
Dawes Close
Churchford Hall
Windmill Hill
Mill Hill
Mill Cl
Days Green
The Street
Cedars Lane
Great Wenham
Wenham Place
Pound Lane
Wenham Lane
Wenham Hill
Old London
Manor House
A12(T)
Oaks Farm
Chaplain's Farm
Lattinford Hill
Four Sisters
A
B
C
D
1
2
3
4
5
607
08
39
38
237
1 grid square represents 500 metres

E
F
G
H
10
11
39
38
237
1
2
3
4
5
Mary
St Mary
Pond Hall
Wood
Broom Way
Hawbridge
Glebe End
Rylands
Longfield
Two Acres
The Squirrels
Road
The Pightle
R Rd
Fr W
Jr Cl
Penn Close
Little Tufts
Great Tufts
Crotchets Close
Penny Meadow
Peter's Grove
Thorney
Boydlands
Shop Precinct
Winding Pc
Barnfield
Garrods
Butchers Lane
Snowcroft
The Street
The Old
PO
Chapel
Link Rd
Tawney Cl
Elm Lane
White Horse Rd
Homefield
Mowlands
Long Perry
Letton Cl
Rembrow
Smithers Close
Stockmers End
Bushey Close
Playfield Road
Friars
London Road
London Rd
Chalkners Cl
Sawyers Close
A12(T)
Red Lane
Bluegate Lane
Tawneys Farm
Potash
Grove Farm
Bentley
Case Lane
The Link
West Mill Garden
Vw Gn
South
East Mill Gn
Station Road
Grove Rd
Link Lane
Dodnash Wood

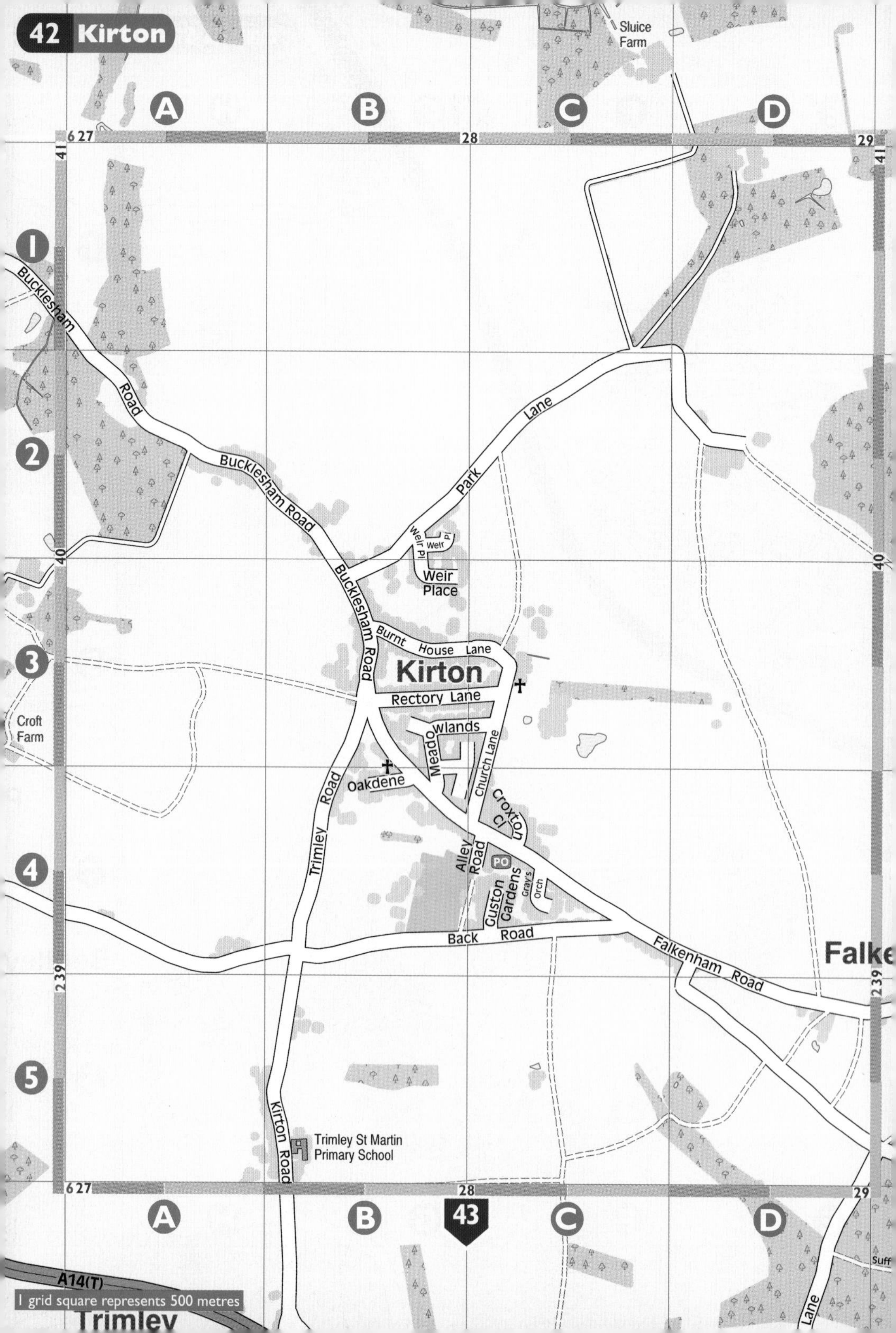
Sluice Farm
A
B
C
D
6 27
28
29
41
40
239
1
2
3
4
5
Bucklesham Road
Bucklesham Road
Bucklesham Road
Park Lane
Weir Pl
Weir Pl
Weir Place
Burnt House Lane
Kirton
Rectory Lane
Meado
wlands
Church Lane
Oakdene
Croxton Cl
Trimley Road
Alley Road
PO
Guston Gardens
Grays Orch
Back Road
Falkenham Road
Falke
Croft Farm
Kirton Road
Trimley St Martin Primary School
43
A14(T)
Lane
Suff
1 grid square represents 500 metres
Trimley

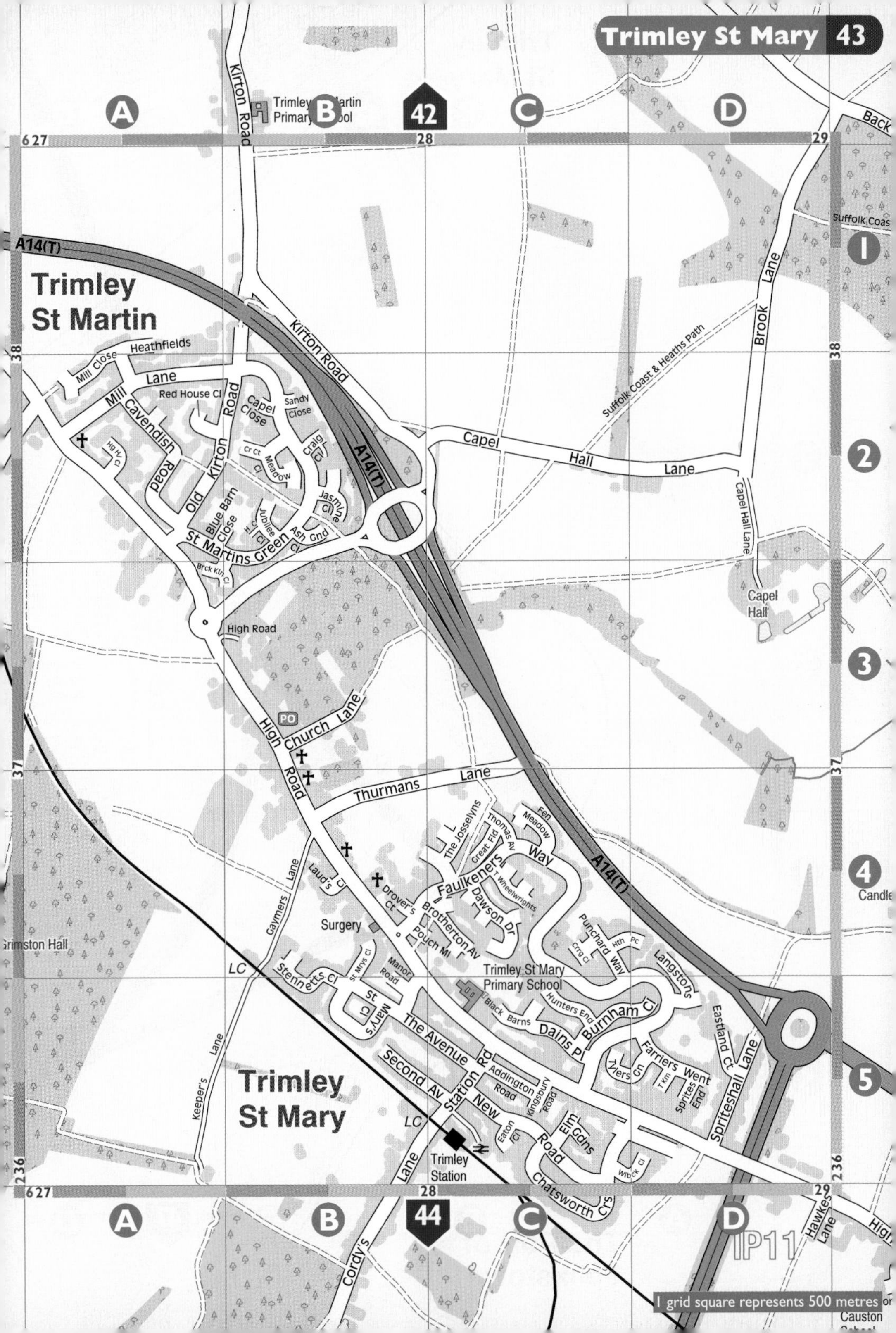
Trimley St Martin
Trimley St Mary
Trimley St Martin Primary School
Trimley St Mary Primary School
Kirton Road
A14(T)
Heathfields
Mill Close
Mill Lane
Red House Cl
Cavendish Road
Old Kirton Road
Capel Close
Sandy Close
Craig Cl
Meadow Cl
Jasmine Cl
Jubilee Cl
Ash Gnd
Blue Barn Close
St Martins Green
High Road
Church Lane
Thurmans Lane
Capel Hall Lane
Brook Lane
Suffolk Coast & Heaths Path
Capel Hall
The Josselyns
Thomas Av
Great Fld
Fen Meadow Way
Faulkeners Way
Dawson Dr
Brotherton Av
Pouch Ml
Drover's Ct
Laud's Cl
Gaymers Lane
Surgery
Grimston Hall
Stennetts Cl
St Mrys Cl
Manor Road
St Mary's Cl
The Avenue
Second Av
Station Rd
Addington Road
Kingsbury Road
New Road
Eaton Cl
Elm Gdns
Chatsworth Crs
Black Barns
Hunters End
Dains Pl
Burnham Cl
Punchard Way
Langstons
Eastland Ct
Spriteshall Lane
Farriers Went
Sprites End
Tylers Gn
Keeper's Lane
Cordy's Lane
Trimley Station
Hawkes Lane
IP11
Candle
Suffolk Coas
Back
High
Causton School
LC
PO
A B C D
1 2 3 4 5
42 44
627 28 29
38 37 236
1 grid square represents 500 metres

1 grid square represents 500 metres

FELIXSTOWE
Walton
CANDLET ROAD
A154
Cowpasture Farm
Treetops
Ascot Drive
Gulpher
Church Lane
Falcon Street
High Street
Surgery
Longcroft
Maidstone Road
Alexandra Rd
King Street
Crown St
Queen St
The Walk
Cage Lane
Graham Rd
Ataka Rd
Recreation La
Exmoor Road
Plymouth Rd
Taunton Road
Exeter Rd
Seaton Road
Infant School
Margaret St
Recreation Gound
Chepstow Rd
Kemsley Rd
Chester Rd
Devon Rd
Back La
West
Candlet Gv
Cornwall Road
GARRISON LA
A1021
GROVE ROAD
Springfield Av
Glenfield Avenue
Fairfield Av
Police Station
Fairfield Infant Sch
BEATRICE AV
Links Avenue
Colneis Road
Colneis Junior School
Lansdowne Road
Rosemary Avenue
Felixstowe & Walton FC
Dellwood Avenue
Fleetwood Avenue
Lynwood Avenue
Sunray Av
Upperfield
Sunningdale Drive
Prestwick Avenue
Wentworth Drive
Gosford
Ferndown Rd
Quinton's Lane
46
High Road
Park Avenue
East
Brackenbury Centre
Pickets Road
Lodge Drive
Foxgrove Gardens
Foxgrove Lane
Felixstowe Station
Gt Eastern Square
Fire Stn
Surg
Shop Cen
Hotel
HAMILTON ROAD A1021
Fleetwood Road
Croutel Road
Allenby Park
Brook Lane
Bridge Road
St Andrew's Road
Walk
Valley
Lawn Wy
Nursery Walk
Shrubbery Cl
Grange Cl
Langley Close
Langley Avenue
Felixstowe Cemetery
Selvale Way
Wadgate Road
Playing Field
Deben High School
Eagles Cl
Princes Road
Cowley Rd
Penfold Rd
Palace
Gainsborough Rd
Constable Road
Quilter Road
Bath Road
Rosebery Rd
Berners Road
Beach East Road
High Beach
Bartlet Hospital
Undercliff Road
York Rd
Felix Rd
Felixstowe General Hospital
Barton Road
The Ct's
Cobbold Road
Newry Av
Goyfield Avenue
Surrey Road
Princes Gdns
Queen's Road
Tomline Road
Cobbold Rd
Cresent Rd
LEOPOLD RD
CRESCENT RD
HIGHFIELD RD
HAMILTON RD
B1082
Victoria Street
Ranelagh Road
Montague Rd
Brownlow Rd
Spa Gardens
Thorn Way
Mill Lane
Mill La
GARRISON LANE
St Johns Court
Princes Rd
Chaucer Rd
Deben Wy
Stour Av
Kings Fleet Rd
Butley Rd
Waveney Rd
Drive
Way
Garfield Rd
Tower Road
A1021 ORWELL RD
BENT HL
Hamilton Gdns
Suffolk Coast & Heaths Path
Spa Pavillion Theatre
Undercliff Rd W
Riby Rd
Bacton Rd
Garfield Rd
Victoria Rd
Wolsey Gardens
South Hill
Town Hall
Lincoln Ter
Charles Road
UNDERCLIFF ROAD WEST
Leisure Cen
Felixstowe Pier
Granville Road
Cavendish Rd
Holland Rd
Russell Rd
Beach Rd W
Road
Htl
Manning Road
Langer Park Industrial Est
Peewit Caravan Park
LANGER ROAD
Buregate Road
Arwela Rd
Marina Gdns
Manwick Rd
Sea
Langer Primary School
St Edmund's Road
Platters Rd
BEACH STATION RD
Orford Road
Tacon Rd
Orford Rd
Pretyman Road
47
E
F
G
H
I
2
3
4
5
30
31
36
35
234

Old Felixstowe
Ferry Road
Cliff Rd
Felixstowe Ferry Golf Club
Golf Course
Fleet House
Park Farm
Kings Fleet Primary School
Felixstowe International College
The Brackenbury Sports Centre
Felixstowe College
Undercliff Road East
Suffolk Coast & Heaths Pth
Gulpher Road
Marsh Lane
Westmorland Road
Western Avenue
St. George's Road
Church Road
Maybush Lane
Golf Road
Cliff Road
Colneis Road
Upperfield Drive
Brinkley Way
Hollybush Dr
Elmcroft Lane
Gosford Way
Foxgrove Lane
Thornley Rd
Pickets Road
Rosebery Rd
Sunningdale Drive
Prestwick Avenue
Looe Road
Quinton's Lane
Marcus Road
Roman Way
Dukes Close
The Pines
45

A154
WALTON AV
Hauliers Road
Station Road
Works
LC
BEACH STATION RD
Langer Primary School
Marina Gdns
Manwick Rd
Micklegate Rd
PO
Beach Station Rd
Levington Road
Nacton Rd
Orford Road
Tacon Rd
Orford Rd
Pretyman Road
Suffolk Coast
LANGER ROAD
CARR ROAD
A154
Manor Rd
Sunderland Rd
Schneider Cl
Darrell Road
Adastra Close
Manor Terrace
View Point Road
Stonegrove Road
Dock Road
Store Road
Cold Store Road
Pier Road
The Docks
Landguard Fort
Nature Reserve
Landguard Point
44
45
A
B
C
D
1
2
3
4
5
628
29
30
33
32
231
1 grid square represents 500 metres

Town/village	Page	Grid
Badley Hill	4	A2
Barham	7	G1
Beacon Hill	15	F2
Belstead	29	G4
Blacksmith's Corner	29	G5
Bramford	10	A3
Brightwell	26	C5
Broke Hall	23	G5
Broom Hill	17	E1
Bucklesham	35	F3
Burgh	27	C1
Burstall	18	C3
California	23	F2
Capel St Mary	40	D2
Castle Hill	11	G2
Chantry	21	E5
Claydon	7	E3
Coddenham Green	5	H2
The Common	6	B5
Copdock	28	D4
Falkenham	42	D4
Felixstowe	45	G4
Gainsborough	32	B3
Gipsy Row	40	B1
Great Blakenham	6	B1
Greenwich	31	F2
Grundisburgh	27	B3
Hadleigh	37	E3
Hintlesham	18	B4
Ipswich	3	G6
Kesgrave	24	D2
Kingston	17	F2
Kirton	42	B3
Lattinford Hill	40	B5
Levington	39	G3
Little Bealings	15	F1
Mace Green	28	B4
Maidenhall	30	D1
Maidensgrave	9	E5
Martlesham	16	A3
Martlesham Heath	26	A2
Melton	9	H1
Mill Hills	9	G2
Nacton	39	E1
Needham Market	4	C3
Old Felixstowe	46	B4
Playford	14	D1
Priory Heath	32	D2
Racecourse	31	H1
Rose Hill	22	D4
Rushmere St Andrew	13	H5
Rushmere Street	14	
Sproughton	20	
Stoke	2	
Stoke Park	30	
Trimley St Martin	43	
Trimley St Mary	43	
Walton	45	
Warren Heath	33	
Washbrook	28	
Washbrook Street	28	
Westbourne	11	
Westerfield	12	
Wherstead	30	
White House	11	
Whitton	10	
Woodbridge	9	

USING THE STREET INDEX

Street names are listed alphabetically. Each street name is followed by its postal town or area locality, the Postcode District, the page number, and the reference to the square in which the name is found.

Standard index entries are shown as follows:

Abbotsbury Cl *CHTY* IP2 ....**30** C2

Street names and selected addresses not shown on the map due to scale restrictions are shown in the index with an asterisk:

Adams Cl *CHTY* * IP2 ....**22** A5

GENERAL ABBREVIATIONS

Abbreviation	Meaning
ACC	ACCESS
ALY	ALLEY
AP	APPROACH
AR	ARCADE
ASS	ASSOCIATION
AV	AVENUE
BCH	BEACH
BLDS	BUILDINGS
BND	BEND
BNK	BANK
BR	BRIDGE
BRK	BROOK
BTM	BOTTOM
BUS	BUSINESS
BVD	BOULEVARD
BY	BYPASS
CATH	CATHEDRAL
CEM	CEMETERY
CEN	CENTRE
CFT	CROFT
CH	CHURCH
CHA	CHASE
CHYD	CHURCHYARD
CIR	CIRCLE
CIRC	CIRCUS
CL	CLOSE
CLFS	CLIFFS
CMP	CAMP
CNR	CORNER
CO	COUNTY
COLL	COLLEGE
COM	COMMON
COMM	COMMISSION
CON	CONVENT
COT	COTTAGE
COTS	COTTAGES
CP	CAPE
CPS	COPSE
CR	CREEK
CREM	CREMATORIUM
CRS	CRESCENT
CSWY	CAUSEWAY
CT	COURT
CTRL	CENTRAL
CTS	COURTS
CTYD	COURTYARD
CUTT	CUTTINGS
CV	COVE
CYN	CANYON
DEPT	DEPARTMENT
DL	DALE
DM	DAM
DR	DRIVE
DRO	DROVE
DRY	DRIVEWAY
DWGS	DWELLINGS
E	EAST
EMB	EMBANKMENT
EMBY	EMBASSY
ESP	ESPLANADE
EST	ESTATE
EX	EXCHANGE
EXPY	EXPRESSWAY
EXT	EXTENSION
F/O	FLYOVER
FC	FOOTBALL CLUB
FK	FORK
FLD	FIELD
FLDS	FIELDS
FLS	FALLS
FLS	FLATS
FM	FARM
FT	FORT
FWY	FREEWAY
FY	FERRY
GA	GATE
GAL	GALLERY
GDN	GARDEN
GDNS	GARDENS
GLD	GLADE
GLN	GLEN
GN	GREEN
GND	GROUND
GRA	GRANGE
GRG	GARAGE
GT	GREAT
GTWY	GATEWAY
GV	GROVE
HGR	HIGHER
HL	HILL
HLS	HILLS
HO	HOUSE
HOL	HOLLOW
HOSP	HOSPITAL
HRB	HARBOUR
HTH	HEATH
HTS	HEIGHTS
HVN	HAVEN
HWY	HIGHWAY
IMP	IMPERIAL
IN	INLET
IND EST	INDUSTRIAL ESTATE
INF	INFIRMARY
INFO	INFORMATION
INT	INTERCHANGE
IS	ISLAND
JCT	JUNCTION
JTY	JETTY
KG	KING
KNL	KNOLL
L	LAKE
LA	LANE
LDG	LODGE
LGT	LIGHT
LK	LOCK
LKS	LAKES
LNDG	LANDING
LTL	LITTLE
LWR	LOWER
MAG	MAGISTRATE
MAN	MANSIONS
MD	MEAD
MDW	MEADOWS
MEM	MEMORIAL
MKT	MARKET
MKTS	MARKETS
ML	MALL
ML	MILL
MNR	MANOR
MS	MEWS
MSN	MISSION
MT	MOUNT
MTN	MOUNTAIN
MTS	MOUNTAINS
MUS	MUSEUM
MWY	MOTORWAY
N	NORTH
NE	NORTH EAST
NW	NORTH WEST
O/P	OVERPASS
OFF	OFFICE
ORCH	ORCHARD
OV	OVAL
PAL	PALACE
PAS	PASSAGE
PAV	PAVILION
PDE	PARADE
PH	PUBLIC HOUSE
PK	PARK
PKWY	PARKWAY
PL	PLACE
PLN	PLAIN
PLNS	PLAINS
PLZ	PLAZA
POL	POLICE STATION
PR	PRINCE
PREC	PRECINCT
PREP	PREPARATORY
PRIM	PRIMARY
PROM	PROMENADE
PRS	PRINCESS
PRT	PORT
PT	POINT
PTH	PATH
PZ	PIAZZA
QD	QUADRANT
QU	QUEEN
QY	QUAY
R	RIVER
RBT	ROUNDABOUT
RD	ROAD
RDG	RIDGE
REP	REPUBLIC
RES	RESERVOIR
RFC	RUGBY FOOTBALL CLUB
RI	RISE
RP	RAMP
RW	ROW
S	SOUTH
SCH	SCHOOL
SE	SOUTH EAST
SER	SERVICE AREA
SH	SHORE
SHOP	SHOPPING
SKWY	SKYWAY
SMT	SUMMIT
SOC	SOCIETY
SP	SPUR
SPR	SPRING
SQ	SQUARE
ST	STREET
STN	STATION
STR	STREAM
STRD	STRAND
SW	SOUTH WEST
TDG	TRADING
TER	TERRACE
THWY	THROUGHWAY
TNL	TUNNEL
TOLL	TOLLWAY
TPK	TURNPIKE
TR	TRACK
TRL	TRAIL
TWR	TOWER
U/P	UNDERPASS
UNI	UNIVERSITY
UPR	UPPER
V	VALE
VA	VALLEY
VIAD	VIADUCT
VIL	VILLA
VIS	VISTA
VLG	VILLAGE
VLS	VILLAS
VW	VIEW
W	WEST
WD	WOOD
WHF	WHARF
WK	WALK
WKS	WALKS
WLS	WELLS
WY	WAY
YD	YARD
YHA	YOUTH HOSTEL

POSTCODE TOWNS AND AREA ABBREVIATIONS

Abbreviation	Meaning
CHTY	Chantry
FRAM/WMKT	Framlingham/ Wickham Market
FX	Felixstowe
HADL	Hadleigh
IP	Ipswich
IPNE	Ipswich northeast
IPSE	Ipswich southeast
KESG	Kesgrave
KIR/NAC	Kirton/Nacton
NHMKT	Needham Market
RCOLE	Rural Colchester east
RIPS/CAP	Rural Ipswich south/ Capel St Ma
RIPW	Rural Ipswich wes
WDBR	Woodbridg

A

otsbury Cl *CHTY* IP2 30 C2
erdeen Wy *IPNE* IP4 13 F4
erfoyle Cl *IPNE* IP4 13 G4
acia Cl *IPSE* IP3 33 E2
er Gv *RIPW* IP8 29 G2
orn Cl *RIPW* IP8 29 G1
con Cl *RIPW* IP8 10 A3
con Gdns *RIPW* IP8 10 A2
con Rd *RIPW* IP8 10 A3
air Rd *IP* IP1 10 D5
ams Cl *CHTY* * IP2 22 A5
ams Pl *KESG* IP5 25 E1
astral Cl *FX* IP11 47 B2
dington Rd *FX* IP11 43 C5
dison Wy *RIPW* IP8 6 C4
elaide Rd *IPNE* IP4 23 H2
ate Cl *IP* IP1 10 D4
slie Rd *IP* IP1 2 A2
thorpe *RIPS/CAP* IP9 40 D2
baster Cl *HADL* IP7 37 E3
n Rd *IPSE* IP3 22 D4
an Sq *WDBR* IP12 16 B3
e Albany *IPNE* IP4 12 C5
erta Cl *KESG* IP5 14 C5
ion Hl *IPNE* IP4 3 K1
ercroft Cl *IP* IP1 11 H2
ercroft Rd *IP* IP1 11 H3
erlee *CHTY* IP2 30 B3
erman Rd *IP* IP1 2 B3
ham Mill Hl *HADL* IP7 36 D1
ham Rd *HADL* IP7 36 D2
ringham Ms *FX* IP11 44 D2
xander Dr *NHMKT* IP6 4 B3
xandra Rd *FX* IP11 45 E1
PNE IP4 3 J2
ce Driver Rd
FRAM/WMKT IP13 27 A3
enby Rd *CHTY* IP2 21 F2
ey Rd *KIR/NAC* IP10 42 B4
ngton Cl *IPNE* IP4 22 D1
Saints' Rd *IP* IP1 21 G1
na Cl *IPNE* IP4 13 E4
nondhayes *CHTY* IP2 21 H5
e St *IP* IP1 2 B1
ton Rd *IPSE* IP3 22 D4
caster Rd *CHTY* IP2 2 B7
derson Cl *NHMKT* IP6 4 B3
derson's Wy *WDBR* IP12 9 E4
drew Cl *FX* IP11 45 E4
dros Cl *IPSE* IP3 32 A4
gela Cl *WDBR* IP12 16 A4
gel La *IPNE* IP4 3 G5
WDBR IP12 9 F3
gel Rd *RIPW* IP8 10 A3
gel St *HADL* IP7 36 D3
glesea Rd *IP* IP1 2 B1
gus Cl *IPNE* IP4 13 F4
ita Cl East *CHTY* IP2 21 E3
ita Cl West *CHTY* IP2 21 E3
n Beaumont Wy *HADL* IP7 36 C2
nbrook Rd *CHTY* IP2 30 A2
ne St *FX* IP11 45 E4
n St *IP* IP1 2 B1
sell Cl *HADL* IP7 36 D3
son Rd *KESG* IP5 16 B5
trim Rd *IP* IP1 10 D4
zani Av *FX* IP11 44 C3
pleby Cl *RIPW* IP8 29 G2
cade St *IP* IP1 2 D3
changel Gdns *CHTY* * IP2 21 E4
e Arches *WDBR* * IP12 9 G3
gyle St *IPNE* IP4 3 G3
kle Ct *KESG* IP5 25 F1
kwright Rd *CHTY* IP2 21 E2
nold Cl *IP* IP1 11 F2
thurs Ter *IPNE* IP4 3 G2
undel Wy *IPSE* IP3 24 A5
wela Rd *FX* IP11 45 F5
cot Dr *FX* IP11 45 E1
PSE IP3 23 F5
hburnham Rd *NHMKT* IP6 4 B4
n Cl *WDBR* IP12 9 F4
ncroft Rd *IP* IP1 11 F4
ndale Rd *KESG* IP5 15 F5
ndown Wy *IPSE* IP3 23 H5
n Ground Cl *FX* IP11 43 B2
n Gv *RIPS/CAP* IP9 41 E2
nley St *CHTY* IP2 2 E7
nmere Gv *IPNE* IP4 3 K2
nton Cl *CHTY* IP2 29 G1
pen Cl *NHMKT* IP6 6 B2
WDBR IP12 9 H2
ter Rd *CHTY* IP2 21 E4
aka Rd *FX* IP11 45 F1
henrye Ct *WDBR* * IP12 9 G4
herton Rd *CHTY* IP2 29 H1
Austin St *CHTY* IP2 2 E6
The Avenue *FX* IP11 43 B5
IP IP1 12 A4
RIPW IP8 28 D4
WDBR IP12 9 G4
Avocet Ct *FX* * IP11 45 F5
Avocet La *KESG* IP5 26 A2
Avondale Rd *IPSE* IP3 32 A1
Aylward Cl *HADL* IP7 37 E5
Ayr Rd *IPNE* IP4 13 F4

B

Back Hamlet *IPSE* IP3 3 H5
Back La *FX* IP11 45 F2
NHMKT IP6 7 E4
RIPW IP8 28 C3
Back Rd *KIR/NAC* IP10 42 B4
Bacon Rd *NHMKT* IP6 7 E3
Bacton Rd *FX* IP11 45 F4
Bader Cl *IPSE* IP3 32 C1
Bader Ct *KESG* IP5 26 A1
Badgers Bank *CHTY* IP2 30 A2
Badley Hl *NHMKT* IP6 4 A1
Badshah Av *IPSE* IP3 23 F5
Bailey Av *KESG* IP5 25 G1
Bailey Cl *CHTY* IP2 21 E2
Baird Cl *CHTY* IP2 21 F1
Bakers La *WDBR* IP12 9 G3
Baldry Cl *RIPW* IP8 29 G2
Ballater Cl *IP* IP1 11 E1
Balmoral Cl *CHTY* IP2 30 B2
Bank Rd *IPNE* IP4 3 J2
Banks Cl *HADL* IP7 37 E4
Bantoft Ter *IPSE* IP3 32 C1
Banyard Cl *KESG* IP5 25 F1
Barker Cl *CHTY* IP2 20 D3
Barking Rd *NHMKT* IP6 4 C5
Barnes Cl *HADL* IP7 37 E3
Barnfield *FX* IP11 44 D1
RIPS/CAP IP9 41 F2
Barnham Pl *KESG* IP5 24 B2
Barons Cl *FX* IP11 46 B3
Baronsdale Cl *IP* IP1 11 H4
Barrack La *IP* IP1 2 C2
Barrack Sq *KESG* IP5 26 B1
Barrett's La *NHMKT* IP6 4 B4
Bartholomew St *IPNE* IP4 3 K3
Barton Cl *CHTY* IP2 30 A1
Barton Rd *FX* IP11 45 H3
WDBR IP12 9 F1
The Barvens *RIPW* IP8 29 E2
Bath Rd *FX* IP11 45 H3
Bath St *CHTY* IP2 22 B5
Battles La *KESG* IP5 25 F1
Bawdsey Cl *FX* IP11 46 B2
Beach Rd East *FX* IP11 46 A5
Beach Rd West *FX* IP11 45 F5
Beach Station Rd *FX* IP11 45 E5
Beacon Fld *FX* IP11 45 E2
Beacon La *FRAM/WMKT* IP13 15 H2
Beaconsfield Rd *IP* IP1 21 F1
WDBR IP12 9 G3
Bealings La
FRAM/WMKT IP13 27 D5
Bealings Rd *WDBR* IP12 16 B2
Beardmore Pk *KESG* IP5 16 B5
Beatrice Av *FX* IP11 45 G1
Beatrice Cl *IPSE* IP3 23 E5
Beatty Rd *IPSE* IP3 32 B1
Beaufort St *IP* IP1 2 A1
Bedford St *IP* IP1 2 C2
Beech Cl *RIPW* IP8 20 A2
Beechcroft Rd *IP* IP1 11 F3
The Beeches *IPSE* IP3 3 K6
NHMKT IP6 7 E4
Beech Gv *IPSE* IP3 22 D5
KESG IP5 24 B1
Beech Rd *KESG* IP5 24 B1
Beech Wy *WDBR* IP12 9 F5
Belgrave Cl *IPNE* IP4 12 C4
Bell Cl *CHTY* IP2 2 E6
Belle Vue Rd *IPNE* IP4 3 J2
Bell La *CHTY* IP2 2 E6
KESG IP5 14 D5
Belmont Rd *RIPW* IP8 29 G2
Belstead Av *CHTY* IP2 21 H5
Belstead Rd *CHTY* IP2 30 B2
Belvedere Rd *IPNE* IP4 12 D5
Benacre Rd *IPSE* IP3 32 A1
Benezet St *IP* IP1 2 B1
Bennett Rd *IP* IP1 10 D5
Bent Hl *FX* IP11 45 G4
Bent La *IPNE* IP4 14 A5
Bentley Rd *IP* IP1 10 C4
Benton St *HADL* IP7 36 D5
Beresford Dr *WDBR* IP12 9 F1
Berkeley Cl *IPNE* IP4 12 C4
Bermuda Rd *KIR/NAC* IP10 33 E4
Bernard Crs *IPSE* IP3 32 B1
Berners Rd *FX* IP11 46 A5
Berners St *IP* IP1 2 C2
Berry Cl *IPSE* IP3 33 F2
Betts Av *KESG* IP5 26 B1
Beverley Rd *IPNE* IP4 12 D5
Bibb Wy *IP* IP1 2 A4
Bilney Rd *WDBR* IP12 9 E3
Birch Cl *WDBR* IP12 9 F5
Birch Gv *KESG* IP5 26 B2
Birchcroft Rd *IP* IP1 11 H3
Birchwood Dr *KESG* IP5 14 A4
Birkfield Cl *CHTY* IP2 21 G4
Birkfield Dr *CHTY* IP2 30 A2
Bishops Cl *FX* IP11 46 B3
Bishop's Hl *IPSE* IP3 3 J6
Bittern Cl *CHTY* IP2 21 E5
Bixley Dr *IPNE* IP4 24 A3
Bixley La *IPNE* IP4 24 B3
Bixley Rd *IPSE* IP3 23 H5
Black Barns *FX* IP11 43 C5
Blackdown Av *KESG* IP5 24 B2
Blackfriars Ct *IPNE* * IP4 3 F4
Black Horse La *IP* IP1 2 D3
Blackthorn Cl *IPSE* IP3 33 E2
Blacktiles La *WDBR* IP12 16 A3
Bladen Dr *IPNE* IP4 24 B3
Blair Cl *IPNE* IP4 24 A3
Blake Rd *IP* IP1 11 F2
Blanche St *IPNE* IP4 3 G3
Blandford Rd *IPSE* IP3 23 H5
Blenheim Rd *IP* IP1 21 G1
Blickling Cl *CHTY* IP2 30 D1
Blofield Rd *FX* IP11 44 C3
Bloomfield St *IPNE* IP4 23 F2
Blue Barn Cl *FX* IP11 43 A2
Blue Barn La *RIPW* IP8 6 B4
Bluebell Cl *CHTY* IP2 21 E4
Bluebell Gv *NHMKT* IP6 4 C5
Bluegate La *RIPS/CAP* IP9 41 E4
Bluestem Rd *IPSE* IP3 32 D3
Blyford Wy *FX* IP11 44 C3
Blyth Cl *CHTY* IP2 30 C2
Bobbits La *RIPS/CAP* IP9 30 A3
Bodiam Cl *IPSE* IP3 23 H4
Bodiam Rd *IPSE* IP3 23 H4
Bodmin Cl *KESG* IP5 24 C2
Bolton La *IPNE* IP4 3 F2
Bond St *IPNE* IP4 3 G4
Bonnington Rd *IPSE* IP3 31 H2
Booth La *KESG* IP5 15 G5
Borrett Pl *WDBR* IP12 8 D5
Borrowdale Av *IPNE* IP4 12 B4
Bosmere Ct *NHMKT* * IP6 4 C4
Boss Hall Rd *IP* IP1 21 E1
Bostock Rd *CHTY* IP2 31 E2
Boston Rd *IPNE* IP4 22 D1
Boswell La *HADL* IP7 36 D2
Boulge Rd *FRAM/WMKT* IP13 27 C1
Bourchier Cl *HADL* IP7 37 E3
Bourne Hl *CHTY* IP2 31 E3
Bowland Dr *RIPW* IP8 29 G2
Bowthorpe Cl *IP* IP1 2 B1
Boxford Ct *FX* IP11 44 C3
Boydlands *RIPS/CAP* IP9 41 E2
Boyton Rd *IPSE* IP3 32 B3
Bracken Av *KESG* IP5 15 G5
Brackenbury Cl *IP* IP1 11 H5
Brackenhayes Cl *CHTY* IP2 21 H5
Brackley Cl *FX* IP11 44 D2
Bradfield Av *HADL* IP7 36 D2
Bradfield Crs *HADL* IP7 36 D2
Bradley St *CHTY* IP2 2 D7
Bramble Dr *IPSE* IP3 33 E2
Bramblewood *RIPW* IP8 29 G1
Bramford La *IP* IP1 10 D4
IP IP1 21 G1
Bramford Rd *IP* IP1 10 C5
NHMKT IP6 6 B3
Bramhall Cl *CHTY* IP2 29 H2
Brandon Rd *FX* IP11 44 C3
Bransby Gdns *IPNE* IP4 3 H1
Brazier's Wood Rd *IPSE* IP3 32 B3
Brecon Cl *CHTY* IP2 30 D1
Bredfield Cl *FX* IP11 44 D2
Bredfield Rd *WDBR* IP12 9 F1
Bredfield St *WDBR* IP12 9 F3
Brendon Dr *KESG* IP5 24 B2
Brett Av *HADL* IP7 37 E2
Brettenham Crs *IP* IP1 12 B4
The Bretts *KESG* IP5 15 G5
Briarhayes Cl *CHTY* IP2 21 H5
Briarwood Rd *WDBR* IP12 9 E5
Brick Kiln Cl *FX* IP11 43 A3
Bridge Rd *FX* IP11 45 G2
KIR/NAC IP10 39 G3
Bridge St *HADL* IP7 36 C3
IP IP1 2 E6
NHMKT IP6 4 C3
Bridgewood Rd *WDBR* IP12 9 E3
Bridgwater Rd *CHTY* IP2 29 H1
Bridport Av *IPSE* IP3 23 H5
Brights Wk *KESG* IP5 25 G1
Brightwell Cl *FX* IP11 44 C3
Brimstone Rd *RIPW* IP8 30 A3
Brinkley Wy *FX* IP11 46 B2
Brisbane Rd *IPNE* IP4 23 H2
Bristol Rd *IPNE* IP4 23 E1
Britannia Rd *IPNE* IP4 23 F2
Broadlands Wy *IPNE* IP4 24 B3
Broad Meadow *RIPW* IP8 29 G1
Broadmere Rd *IP* IP1 11 E5
Brock La *FRAM/WMKT* IP13 16 C1
Brockley Crs *IP* IP1 10 D4
Broke Av *RIPW* IP8 10 B3
Broke Hall Gdns *IPSE* IP3 23 H4
Bromeswell Rd *IPNE* IP4 12 C4
Bromley Cl *CHTY* IP2 22 A5
Brookfield Rd *IP* IP1 11 F5
Brookhill Wy *IPNE* IP4 24 B4
Brook La *FX* IP11 45 H2
KIR/NAC IP10 43 D1
NHMKT IP6 14 C1
RIPS/CAP IP9 40 C1
Brooks Hall Rd *IP* IP1 21 G1
Brook St *WDBR* IP12 9 G3
Brookview *CHTY* IP2 30 A2
Broom Crs *IPSE* IP3 31 H2
Broom Fld *FX* IP11 45 E2
Broomfield *KESG* IP5 25 H1
Broomfield Common
RIPW IP8 20 B2
Broomfield Ms *KESG* IP5 26 A1
Broomhayes *CHTY* IP2 30 C1
Broomheath *WDBR* IP12 17 F1
Broom Hill Rd *IP* IP1 11 G5
Broom Wy *RIPS/CAP* IP9 41 E1
Brotherton Av *FX* IP11 43 B4
Broughton Rd *IP* IP1 21 H1
Browning Rd *IP* IP1 11 F2
Brownlow Rd *FX* IP11 45 G3
Browns Gv *KESG* IP5 25 F1
Brunel Rd *CHTY* IP2 21 E2
Brunskill Pl *HADL* * IP7 36 C2
Brunswick Rd *IPNE* IP4 22 D1
Bryon Av *FX* IP11 44 B5
Buckenham Rd *HADL* IP7 37 F5
Buckfast Cl *CHTY* IP2 30 C1
Buckingham Cl *WDBR* IP12 16 A3
Bucklesham Rd *IPSE* IP3 32 D1
KIR/NAC IP10 42 A2
Buck's Head La *NHMKT* IP6 5 H2
Buck's Horns La *RIPW* IP8 29 F4
Buddleia Cl *CHTY* IP2 21 E4
Bude Cl *KESG* IP5 24 C2
Bugsby Wy *KESG* IP5 25 G1
Bullard's La *WDBR* IP12 9 E3
Bullen Cl *RIPW* IP8 10 A3
Bullen La *RIPW* IP8 10 A3
Bulls Cliff *FX* * IP11 45 F4
Bulstrode Rd *CHTY* IP2 3 F6
Bulwer Rd *IP* IP1 2 A2
The Bungalows
KIR/NAC * IP10 38 D2
Bunting Rd *CHTY* IP2 20 D5
Bunyan Cl *IP* IP1 11 G2
Buregate Rd *FX* IP11 45 F5
Burgess Pl *KESG* IP5 26 B1
Burghley Cl *CHTY* IP2 30 C1
Burke Cl *IP* IP1 11 F2
Burke Rd *IP* IP1 11 G2
Burkitt Rd *WDBR* IP12 9 F3
Burlington Rd *IP* IP1 2 B3
Burnet Cl *RIPW* IP8 29 H3
Burnham Cl *FX* IP11 43 C5
IPNE IP4 22 D1
Burns Rd *IP* IP1 11 E2
Burnt House La *KIR/NAC* IP10 42 B3
Burrell Rd *CHTY* IP2 2 C6
Burstall Hall La *RIPW* IP8 18 D2
Burstall La *RIPW* IP8 19 E3
Burton Dr *NHMKT* IP6 4 B3
Bury Hl *WDBR* IP12 9 G1
Bury Hill Cl *WDBR* IP12 9 G1
Bury Rd *IP* IP1 10 D1
Bushey Cl *RIPS/CAP* IP9 41 E2
Bushman Gdns *RIPW* IP8 10 A3
Butchers La *RIPS/CAP* IP9 41 F2
Butler Smith Gdns *KESG* IP5 25 E1
Butley Cl *CHTY* IP2 30 B3
Butley Rd *FX* IP11 45 E4
Buttercup Cl *RIPW* IP8 29 G2
Butterfly Gdns *IPNE* IP4 24 A3
Buttermarket *IP* IP1 2 E3
Byland Cl *CHTY* IP2 30 C1
Byron Rd *IP* IP1 11 E1

C

Cage La *FX* IP11 45 E2
Caithness Cl *IPNE* IP4 13 F5
Calais St *HADL* IP7 36 D3
California *WDBR* IP12 8 D5
Camberley Rd *IPNE* IP4 23 H1
Camborne Rd *KESG* IP5 24 D1
Cambridge Dr *CHTY* IP2 30 A2
Cambridge Rd *FX* IP11 45 H3
KESG IP5 14 C5
Camden Rd *IPSE* IP3 23 F4
Campbell Rd *IPSE* IP3 32 C2
Campion Rd *CHTY* IP2 21 F4
Camwood Gdns *IPSE* IP3 23 F4
Canberra Cl *IPNE* IP4 23 H2
Candlet Gv *FX* IP11 45 F2
Canham St *IP* IP1 2 C3
Canterbury Cl *CHTY* IP2 30 B3
Canterbury Gdns *HADL* IP7 37 E3
Capel Cl *FX* IP11 43 B2
Capel Dr *FX* IP11 44 C3
Capel Hall La *FX* IP11 43 D2
Carders Cl *HADL* IP7 37 E5
Cardew Drift *KESG* IP5 15 F5
Cardiff Av *CHTY* IP2 30 D2
Cardigan St *IP* IP1 2 B1
Cardinal St *IP* IP1 2 D5
Carlford Cl *KESG* IP5 26 A1
Carlton Rd *KESG* IP5 24 C1
Carlton Wk *HADL* IP7 37 E5
Carlton Wy *IPNE* IP4 12 C5
Carlyle Cl *IP* IP1 11 F1
Carmarthen Cl *CHTY* IP2 30 C2
Carol Av *WDBR* IP12 16 A4
Carolbrook Rd *CHTY* IP2 30 A2
Carol Cl *FX* IP11 46 A4
Carriage Cl *FX* IP11 43 C4
Carr Rd *FX* IP11 47 B2
Carr St *IPNE* IP4 3 F3
Case La *RIPS/CAP* IP9 41 H5
Castle Cl *FX* IP11 46 B3
Castle La *HADL* IP7 36 C2
Castle Ri *HADL* IP7 36 B2
Castle Rd *HADL* IP7 36 B2
IP IP1 11 E4
Castle St *WDBR* IP12 9 F3
Catesbray *RIPS/CAP* IP9 40 D2
Catherine Rd *WDBR* IP12 9 E2
Cauldwell Av *IPNE* IP4 22 D2
Cauldwell Hall Rd *IPNE* IP4 23 E1
The Causeway *NHMKT* IP6 4 C4
Cavan Rd *IP* IP1 10 D3
Cavendish Rd *FX* IP11 43 A2
FX IP11 45 F4
Cavendish St *IPSE* IP3 3 K6
Cecilia St *IP* IP1 2 D5
Cecil Rd *IP* IP1 2 C2
Cedar Av *KESG* IP5 24 C2
Cedarcroft Rd *IP* IP1 11 F3
Cedars La *RIPS/CAP* IP9 40 D2
Cemetery La *IPNE* IP4 12 C5
WDBR IP12 9 E4
Cemetery Rd *IPNE* IP4 3 G2
Central Av *IPSE* IP3 32 D3
Century Dr *KESG* IP5 25 G1
Chainhouse Rd *NHMKT* IP6 4 C4
Chalkeith Rd *NHMKT* IP6 4 D5
Chalk Hill La *NHMKT* IP6 6 A2
Chalkners Cl *RIPS/CAP* IP9 41 E2
Chalon St *IP* IP1 2 C4
Chamberlain Wy *RIPW* IP8 29 G1
Chandos Ct *WDBR* IP12 16 A3
Chandos Dr *WDBR* IP12 16 A3
Chantry Gn *CHTY* IP2 20 D5
Chantry Pk *CHTY* * IP2 20 D3
Chapel Cl *RIPS/CAP* IP9 41 E2
Chapel Fld *RIPW* IP8 10 A3
Chapel La *FRAM/WMKT* IP13 27 B4
NHMKT IP6 6 C4
RIPW IP8 29 E2
RIPW IP8 29 G4
Chapel Rd *FRAM/WMKT* IP13 27 B4
Chapel St *WDBR* IP12 9 G3
Charles Av *FRAM/WMKT* IP13 27 A3
Charles Rd *FX* IP11 45 E4
Charles St *IP* IP1 2 D2
Charlotte's *RIPW* IP8 28 D2
Charlton Av *IP* IP1 11 F3
Chartwell Cl *IPNE* IP4 23 E3
The Chase *KESG* IP5 26 A1
Chatsworth Crs *CHTY* IP2 30 C1
FX IP11 43 C5
Chatsworth Dr *IPNE* IP4 24 A3
Chaucer Rd *FX* IP11 45 F4
IP IP1 11 F2
Chelsea Cl *IP* IP1 11 F4
Chelsworth Av *IPNE* IP4 12 B4
Chelsworth Rd *FX* IP11 44 D4
Cheltenham Av *IP* IP1 11 H4
Chepstow Rd *FX* IP11 45 F2
IP IP1 11 H1
Chequers Ri *NHMKT* IP6 6 B2
Cherry Blossom Cl *RIPW* IP8 29 F1
Cherry Gardens La *IPNE* IP4 23 F1
Cherry Tree Rd *WDBR* IP12 9 F4
Cherry Wd *RIPW* * IP8 28 D4
Chesapeake Rd *IPSE* IP3 32 A3
Chesham Rd *CHTY* IP2 2 C7
Chessington Gdns *IP* IP1 11 F5
Chesterfield Dr *IP* IP1 11 F3
Chester Rd *FX* IP11 45 F2
Chesterton Cl *CHTY* IP2 30 B2
Chestnut Cl *KESG* IP5 14 A4
Chestnut Dr *NHMKT* IP6 7 E4
The Chestnuts *CHTY* IP2 29 G1
Chevalier Rd *FX* IP11 45 H3
Chevallier St *IP* IP1 21 G1
Childers Fld *FX* IP11 44 D2
Chilton Rd *IPSE* IP3 23 G4
Christchurch Ct *IPNE* * IP4 3 G2
Christchurch Dr *WDBR* IP12 8 D5
Christchurch St *IPNE* IP4 3 G1
Church Cl *KESG* IP5 14 D5
KIR/NAC IP10 35 E2
RCOLE * CO7 40 A2
Church Crs *RIPW* IP8 20 A2
Church Gn *RIPW* IP8 10 B4
Church Hl *RIPW* IP8 18 D2
Churchill Av *HADL* IP7 36 D2
IPNE IP4 23 F3
Churchill Cl *WDBR* IP12 9 E4
Church La *FX* IP11 43 B3
FX IP11 45 E1
KIR/NAC IP10 35 E2
KIR/NAC IP10 39 G3
KIR/NAC IP10 42 C4
NHMKT IP6 4 C1
NHMKT IP6 7 F4
NHMKT IP6 7 E2
NHMKT IP6 12 D1
NHMKT IP6 14 D1
RIPW IP8 20 B3
RIPW IP8 28 B3
RIPW IP8 29 E4
WDBR IP12 16 D3
Church Rd *FRAM/WMKT* IP13 8 B1
FX IP11 46 A3
KIR/NAC IP10 38 D2
Church St *HADL* IP7 36 D3
WDBR IP12 9 G3
Civic Dr *IP* IP1 2 C3
Clapgate La *IPSE* IP3 23 E5
Clare Av *WDBR* IP12 9 E4
Clarence Rd *IPSE* IP3 32 B2
Clare Rd *IPNE* IP4 12 D5
Clarkson St *IP* IP1 2 B2
Claude St *IP* IP1 2 D2
Claverton Wy *IPNE* IP4 23 H3
Clayton Ct *WDBR* IP12 8 D5
Clench Cl *IPNE* IP4 3 G3
Cliff La *IPSE* IP3 22 D5
Clifford Rd *IPNE* IP4 3 K4
Cliff Rd *FX* IP11 46 B4
IPSE IP3 22 C5
Clifton Wy *CHTY* IP2 29 H1
Clive Av *IP* IP1 11 H3
Cloncurry Gdns *FX* IP11 44 D4
Clopton Gdns *HADL* IP7 36 D4
Clovelly Cl *IPNE* IP4 24 B4
Clover Cl *CHTY* IP2 21 F4
NHMKT IP6 4 C5
Clump Fld *CHTY* * IP2 30 B1
Coachmans Ct *IPNE* * IP4 2 E4
Cobbold Ms *IPNE* IP4 3 G2
Cobbold Rd *FX* IP11 45 H3
WDBR IP12 9 E1
Cobbold St *IPNE* IP4 3 F2
Cobden Pl *IPNE* IP4 3 G3
Cobham Rd *IPSE* IP3 32 C1
Coddenham Rd *NHMKT* IP6 4 D4
Cody Rd *IPSE* IP3 32 C2
Colchester Rd *IPNE* IP4 12 D4
Cold Store Rd *FX* IP11 44 C5
Cole Ness Rd *IPSE* IP3 32 A3
Coleridge Rd *IP* IP1 11 F2
College St *IPSE* IP3 2 E5
Collett's Wk *WDBR* IP12 9 E3
Collingwood Av *IPSE* IP3 32 B1
Collingwood Rd *WDBR* IP12 9 F1
Collinson's *CHTY* IP2 20 C3
Colneis Rd *FX* IP11 45 G1
Coltsfoot Rd *CHTY* IP2 21 E4
Columbia Cl *KESG* IP5 24 C1
Columbine Gdns *CHTY* IP2 21 E3
Commercial Rd *IP* IP1 2 C6
Common Quay *IPSE* * IP3 3 F5
Conach Rd *WDBR* IP12 9 E3
Congreve Rd *IP* IP1 11 G2
Coniston Cl *FX* IP11 46 C2
Coniston Rd *IPSE* IP3 32 B1
Connaught Rd *IP* IP1 10 D3
Constable Rd *FX* IP11 45 H3
IPNE IP4 22 B1
Constantine Rd *IP* IP1 2 B5
Constitution Hl *IP* IP1 11 H5
NHMKT IP6 4 C3
Convalescent Hl *FX* IP11 45 G4
Conway Cl *CHTY* IP2 30 D1
FX IP11 46 A2
Cooks Cl *KESG* IP5 15 G5
Coombers *RIPS/CAP* IP9 40 D2
Cooper's Rd *KESG* IP5 26 B1
NHMKT IP6 7 G1
Coopers Wy *NHMKT* IP6 6 D3
Copleston Rd *IPNE* IP4 23 F3
Copperfield Rd *CHTY* IP2 21 E3
Coppice Cl *WDBR* IP12 9 G2
Coprolite St *IPSE* IP3 3 H5
Copswood Cl *KESG* IP5 25 H1
Coral Dr *IP* IP1 10 D4
Coram St *HADL* IP7 36 A3
Corder Rd *IPNE* IP4 12 B5
Cordy's La *FX* IP11 44 B1
Corks La *HADL* IP7 36 C3
Cornflower Cl *CHTY* IP2 21 E4
Cornhill *IP* * IP1 2 D3
Cornwall Rd *FX* IP11 45 E2
Coronation Dr *FX* IP11 44 D4
Coronation Rd *IPNE* IP4 23 F3
Corporation Av *CHTY* IP2 30 C3
Corton Rd *IPSE* IP3 32 B2
Cotman Rd *IPSE* IP3 32 A2
Cotswold Av *IP* IP1 11 H4
Cottesford Cl *HADL* IP7 37 E4
Cottingham Rd *RIPW* IP8 29 F2
The Courts *FX* IP11 45 H3
Cowell St *CHTY* IP2 22 A5
Cowley Rd *FX* IP11 45 G3
Cowper St *IPNE* IP4 23 F2
Cowslip Cl *CHTY* IP2 21 E3
Cowslip Wy *NHMKT* IP6 4 C5
Cox La *IPNE* IP4 3 F4
Coytes Gdns *IP* IP1 2 D4
Crabbe St *IPNE* IP4 23 E2
Craig Cl *FX* IP11 43 B2
Cranborne Cha *IPNE* IP4 13 E4
Crane Cl *WDBR* IP12 8 D5
Cranfield Pk *RIPW* IP8 18 D3
Cranwell Crs *IPSE* IP3 32 C2
Cranwell Gv *KESG* IP5 25 E1
Cranworth Rd *HADL* IP7 37 E5
Crawford La *KESG* IP5 25 E1
The Crescent *NHMKT* IP6 6 C1
Crescent Rd *FX* IP11 45 G3
IP IP1 2 B2
Cricket Hill Rd *FX* IP11 44 D2
Crocus Cl *CHTY* IP2 21 E4
Crofton Rd *IPNE* IP4 23 F1
Croft St *CHTY* IP2 22 A5
Cromarty Rd *IPNE* IP4 13 F5
Cromer Rd *IP* IP1 11 F5
Crompton Rd *CHTY* IP2 21 E1
Cromwell Sq *IP* IP1 2 D4
Crossgate Fld *FX* IP11 45 E2
Crossley Gdns *IP* IP1 10 C3
Cross St *FX* IP11 45 E1
Crotchets Cl *RIPS/CAP* IP9 41 E2
Croutel Rd *FX* IP11 45 H2
Crowland Cl *CHTY* IP2 30 C1
Crowley Rd *NHMKT* IP6 4 C3
Crown & Anchor Ms *IP* * IP1 2 D2
Crown Cl *WDBR* IP12 16 B3
Crown Paddock *NHMKT* * IP6 4 C3
Crown Pl *WDBR* IP12 9 G4
Crown St *FX* IP11 45 E2
IP IP1 2 D2
NHMKT IP6 4 C3
Crowswell Ct *FX* IP11 43 B2
Croxton Cl *KIR/NAC* IP10 42 C4
Cuckfield Av *IPSE* IP3 24 A5
Culford Wk *FX* IP11 44 C4
Cullingham Rd *IP* IP1 21 G2
Cumberland Cl *FX* IP11 46 B3
Cumberland Ms *WDBR* IP12 9 G4
Cumberland St *IP* IP1 2 B1
WDBR IP12 9 G4
Curlew Rd *CHTY* IP2 20 D5
Curriers' La *IP* IP1 2 C4
Curtis Cl *RIPW* IP8 29 G2
Cutler St *IP* IP1 2 D5

D

Daffodil Cl *CHTY* IP2 21 E5
Daimler Rd *IP* IP1 10 C3
Dains Pl *FX* IP11 43
Dale Hall La *IP* IP1 11
Dales Rd *IP* IP1 11
Dales Vw *RIPW* IP8 28
Dales View Rd *IP* IP1 11
Dalton Rd *IP* IP1 2
Damselfly Rd *IPSE* IP3 32
Dandalan Cl *IP* IP1 21
Darrell Rd *FX* IP11 47
Darsham Cl *FX* IP11 44
Darter Cl *IPSE* IP3 32
Darwin Rd *IPNE* IP4 22
Dashwood Cl *RIPW* IP8 29
Daundy Cl *CHTY* IP2 20
Davey Cl *IPSE* IP3 31
Dawes Cl *RIPS/CAP* IP9 40
Dawson Drift *KESG* IP5 25
Dawson Dr *FX* IP11 43
Days Gn *RIPS/CAP* IP9 40
Days Rd *RIPS/CAP* IP9 40
Deacon Ct *FX* IP11 46
Deben Av *KESG* IP5 15
Deben Rd *IP* IP1 11
WDBR IP12 9
Deben Valley Dr *KESG* IP5 25
Deben Wy *FX* IP11 45
De Brink-on-the-Green
KESG * IP5 26
Dedham Pl *IPNE* * IP4 3
Defoe Rd *IP* IP1 11
Delf Cl *HADL* IP7 37
Dellwood Av *FX* IP11 45
Demesne Gdns *KESG* IP5 16
Denton Cl *CHTY* IP2 29
Derby Cl *IPNE* IP4 23
Derby Rd *IPSE* IP3 23
Dereham Av *IPSE* IP3 22
Derwent Rd *IPSE* IP3 22
Devlin Rd *RIPW* IP8 29
Devon Rd *FX* IP11 45
Devonshire Rd *IPSE* IP3 3
Dewar La *KESG* IP5 25
Dhobi Pl *IP* IP1 21
Dial La *IP* IP1 2
Diamond Cl *IP* IP1 10
Dickens Rd *CHTY* IP2 21
Dickinson Ter *KESG* IP5 25
Didsbury Cl *CHTY* IP2 29
Digby Cl *KESG* IP5 26
Digby Rd *IPNE* IP4 23
Dillwyn St *IP* IP1 2
Dillwyn St West *IP* IP1 2
Ditchingham Gv *IPNE* IP4 24
Dobbs Drift *KESG* IP5 25
Dobbs La *KESG* IP5 15
KIR/NAC IP10 25
Dock Basin *FX* * IP11 47
Dock Rd *FX* IP11 47
The Docks *FX* IP11 47
Dock St *CHTY* IP2 2
Doctor Watson's La *KESG* IP5 14
Dodmans *RIPS/CAP* IP9 41
Dodson V *KESG* IP5 25
Dogs Head St *IPNE* IP4 2
Dombey Rd *CHTY* IP2 21
Donegal Rd *IP* IP1 10
Dooley Rd *FX* IP11 44
Dorchester Rd *IPSE* IP3 23
Doric Pl *WDBR* IP12 9
Dorset Cl *IPNE* IP4 12
Dovedale *FX* IP11 44
Dover Rd *IPSE* IP3 23
Dove St *IPNE* IP4 3
Downing Cl *CHTY* IP2 30
WDBR IP12 9
The Downs *FX* IP11 44
Downside Cl *CHTY* IP2 30
Drake Av *IPSE* IP3 32
Drake Sq North *IPSE* IP3 23
Drake Sq South *IPSE* IP3 32
Drapers Cl *HADL* IP7 37
The Drift *FX* * IP11 43
IPNE IP4 23
IPSE IP3 32
KESG IP5 26
Drift Cottages *FX* * IP11 46
The Driftway
FRAM/WMKT IP13 27
IPNE IP4 23
Drover's Ct *FX* IP11 43
Drury Rd *NHMKT* IP6 7
Drybridge Hl *WDBR* IP12 9
Dryden Rd *IP* IP1 11
Duckamere *RIPW* IP8 10
Dukes Cl *FX* IP11 46
Duke's Meadow *WDBR* IP12 8
Duke's Pk *WDBR* IP12 16
Duke St *HADL* IP7 36
IPSE IP3 3
Dumbarton Rd *IPNE* IP4 13

lin Rd *CHTY* IP2 30 A1
lop Rd *CHTY* IP2 21 F2
n Cl *HADL* IP7 37 E4
nton Gv *HADL* IP7 36 D5
er Ct *HADL* IP7 37 F4
ke St *IP* IP1 2 D1

E

gles Cl *FX* IP11 45 F3
gle St *IPNE* IP4 3 F4
gle Wy *KESG* IP5 16 A5
rls Cl *FX* IP11 46 B3
stcliff *FX* IP11 46 C2
stern Cl *IPNE* IP4 24 B4
stland Ct *FX* IP11 43 D5
st Lawn *IPNE* IP4 13 G5
ton Cl *FX* IP11 43 C5
ton Gdns *FX* IP11 45 E5
cles Rd *CHTY* IP2 29 H1
dowes Rd *NHMKT* IP6 7 E3
en Rd *IPNE* IP4 23 F3
geworth Rd *CHTY* IP2 30 A1
nburgh Gdns *NHMKT* IP6 7 E3
monton Cl *KESG* IP5 24 C1
monton Rd *KESG* IP5 14 C5
ward Cl *IP* IP1 11 F5
win Av *WDBR* IP12 9 F1
win Panks Rd *HADL* IP7 37 E3
glestone Cl *CHTY* IP2 30 B2
zabeth Wy *FX* IP11 44 D4
enbrook Rd *CHTY* IP2 29 H2
iott St *IP* IP1 2 A2
ncroft La *FX* IP11 46 A2
ncroft Rd *IP* IP1 11 G3
ners La *KESG* IP5 25 F1
n Gdns *FX* IP11 43 C5
nham Dr *KIR/NAC* IP10 33 H3
nhurst Ct *WDBR* * IP12 9 H3
nhurst Dr *IPSE* IP3 22 D5
n La *RIPS/CAP* IP9 41 E2
RIPW IP8 28 C3
n Rd *KESG* IP5 24 B1
n St *IP* IP1 2 D3
mere Rd *IP* IP1 12 A5
on Pk *CHTY* IP2 20 D2
Rd *IPNE* IP4 12 D4
NHMKT IP6 7 E3
nerald Cl *KESG* IP5 15 E5
nlen St *IP* IP1 2 A3
nmanuel Cl *CHTY* IP2 30 B1
nerdale Cl *FX* IP11 46 B2
som Dr *IP* IP1 11 H1
nleigh Rd *IPNE* IP4 23 F2
sex Wy *IPSE* IP3 33 E2
tuary Dr *FX* IP11 46 B2
ropa Wy *IP* IP1 10 C5
stace Rd *IP* IP1 11 E5
ston Av *IPNE* IP4 24 B2
ston Ct *FX* IP11 44 C3
abrook Cl *CHTY* IP2 30 A2
erton Crs *IP* IP1 11 F4
esham Cl *CHTY* IP2 30 C1
eter Rd *FX* IP11 45 F2
IPSE IP3 23 F4
NHMKT IP6 7 F3
moor Rd *FX* IP11 45 F1

F

gbury Rd *FX* IP11 44 A3
irbairn Av *KESG* IP5 25 F1
irfax Gdns *NHMKT* IP6 4 D4
irfield Av *FX* IP11 45 G2
irfield Rd *IPSE* IP3 32 A1
e Fairways *IPNE* IP4 24 A3
lcon St *FX* IP11 45 E1
IP IP1 2 D4
lkenham Rd *KIR/NAC* IP10 42 C4
lmouth Cl *KESG* IP5 24 D2
raday Rd *IPSE* IP3 22 D3
rina Cl *IP* IP1 21 F1
rlingayes *WDBR* IP12 9 E1
rriers Cl *KESG* IP5 16 A5
rriers Went *FX* IP11 45 D5
rthing Rd *IP* IP1 10 C5
rthings Went *RIPS/CAP* IP9 41 F1
ulkeners Wy *FX* IP11 43 C4
wley Cl *IPNE* IP4 23 G1
yrefield Rd *WDBR* IP12 9 H1
athers Fld *FX* IP11 44 D2
law St *CHTY* IP2 3 F7
lix Cl *KESG* IP5 24 D1
lix Rd *FX* IP11 45 H3
IPSE IP3 32 C1
elixstowe Rd *IPSE* IP3 23 E4
KIR/NAC IP10 34 C5
WDBR IP12 16 B4
Fellbrigg Av *KESG* IP5 24 B2
Fen Meadow *FX* IP11 43 C4
Fentons Wy *KESG* IP5 25 F1
Fen Vw *RIPW* IP8 28 C3
Ferndown Rd *FX* IP11 46 A3
Fernhayes Cl *CHTY* IP2 21 G5
Fernhill Cl *WDBR* IP12 9 G1
Ferry La *FX* IP11 44 D4
Ferry Rd *FX* IP11 46 A2
Field Vw *KIR/NAC* IP10 35 E3
Fife Rd *IPNE* IP4 13 F4
Finbars Wk *IPNE* IP4 3 K4
Finborough Cl *KESG* IP5 24 B2
Finchley Rd *IPNE* IP4 3 H2
Finney's Drift *KIR/NAC* IP10 39 E1
Fircroft Rd *IP* IP1 11 G3
Firefly Wy *IPSE* IP3 32 B2
Fir Tree Ri *RIPW* IP8 29 G1
Fishbane Cl *IPSE* IP3 32 A3
Fitzgerald Rd *WDBR* IP12 9 G2
Fitzmaurice Rd *IPSE* IP3 23 F5
Fitzroy St *IP* IP1 2 E2
Fitzwilliam Cl *CHTY* IP2 30 B1
WDBR IP12 9 E4
Fleetwood Av *FX* IP11 45 G2
Fleetwood Rd *FX* IP11 45 H2
Fletcher Cl *NHMKT* IP6 6 D3
Fletcher Rd *IPSE* IP3 32 A3
Fletchers La *KESG* IP5 15 F5
Flindell Dr *RIPW* IP8 10 A3
Flint Cl *CHTY* IP2 30 D1
Flordon Rd *NHMKT* IP6 4 D2
Foden Av *IP* IP1 10 C3
Fonnereau Rd *IP* IP1 2 D1
Fordham Pl *IPNE* IP4 24 B3
Fore Hamlet *IPSE* IP3 3 H5
Forester Cl *RIPW* IP8 29 H3
Foresters Wk *NHMKT* IP6 6 D3
Forest La *KESG* IP5 26 A2
Fore St *IPNE* IP4 3 F4
Forfar Cl *IPNE* IP4 13 F4
Forge Cl *KIR/NAC* IP10 35 E2
Foundation St *IPNE* IP4 3 F5
Foundry La *IPSE* IP3 2 E5
Fountains Rd *CHTY* IP2 30 B2
Foxglove Av *NHMKT* IP6 4 C5
Foxglove Crs *IPSE* IP3 33 E2
Foxgrove Gdns *FX* IP11 46 A4
Foxgrove La *FX* IP11 46 A4
Foxhall Rd *IPNE* IP4 3 K5
KIR/NAC IP10 25 F3
Fox Lea *KESG* IP5 15 G5
Foxtail Rd *IPSE* IP3 32 D3
Foxwood Crs *IPNE* IP4 24 B3
Frampton Rd *IPSE* IP3 32 A3
Franciscan Wy *IP* IP1 2 D4
Francis Cl *KESG* IP5 15 G5
Franklin Rd *IPSE* IP3 32 B1
Fraser Rd *IP* IP1 21 F1
RIPW IP8 10 B2
Freehold Rd *IPNE* IP4 23 E2
NHMKT IP6 4 B2
Freeman Cl *HADL* IP7 36 D2
Friars *RIPS/CAP* IP9 41 F3
Friars Bridge Rd *IP* IP1 2 C4
Friars Cl *FX* IP11 46 B3
Friars Rd *HADL* IP7 36 C3
Friars St *IP* IP1 2 D4
Friends Wk *KESG* IP5 15 F5
Fritton Cl *CHTY* IP2 30 C2
Frobisher Rd *IPSE* IP3 31 G2
Frog Hall La *HADL* IP7 37 E3
Front Rd *IPSE* IP3 32 D3
Fuchsia La *IPNE* IP4 23 E3
Fullers Cl *HADL* IP7 37 E3
Fullers Fld *NHMKT* * IP6 12 C1
Furness Cl *CHTY* IP2 30 B3
Fynn Rd *WDBR* IP12 8 D5
Fynn Valley Wk *NHMKT* IP6 14 B1

G

Gaell Crs *HADL* IP7 36 D4
Gainsborough La *IPSE* IP3 31 H3
Gainsborough Rd *FX* IP11 45 G3
IPNE IP4 12 B5
Gallows Hl *HADL* IP7 36 C2
Galway Av *IP* IP1 11 E4
Gannet Rd *CHTY* IP2 21 E5
Garden Fld *FX* IP11 45 E2
Garfield Cl *FX* IP11 45 F4
Garfield Rd *FX* IP11 45 F4
Garrick Wy *IP* IP1 11 G2
Garrison La *FX* IP11 45 F4
Garrods *RIPS/CAP* IP9 41 F2
Gatacre Rd *IP* IP1 21 G1
Gaye St *IP* IP1 2 B2
Gayfer Av *KESG* IP5 15 H5
Gaymers La *FX* IP11 43 B4
Generals Ms *FX* IP11 44 D2
Geneva Av *KESG* IP5 16 C5
Geneva Rd *IP* IP1 2 C2
George Frost Cl *IPNE* IP4 22 B1
George St *HADL* IP7 37 E3
RIPW IP8 18 B5
Geralds Av *IPNE* IP4 23 E3
Gibbons St *IP* IP1 2 A3
Giffords Pl *IPNE* IP4 24 B2
Gilbert Cl *NHMKT* IP6 4 B3
Giles Ct *NHMKT* * IP6 7 E3
Gippeswyk Av *CHTY* IP2 2 A7
Gippeswyk Rd *CHTY* IP2 2 B7
Gipping Rd *NHMKT* IP6 6 C3
Gippingstone Rd *RIPW* IP8 10 A4
Gipping Valley River Pth
NHMKT IP6 6 B1
RIPW IP8 10 A2
Gipping Wy *RIPW* IP8 10 A3
RIPW IP8 20 B2
Gipsy La *NHMKT* IP6 4 B2
Girton Cl *WDBR* IP12 8 D4
Girton Wy *CHTY* IP2 30 B2
Gladstone Rd *IPSE* IP3 3 K5
WDBR IP12 9 G3
Glamorgan Rd *CHTY* IP2 30 D2
Glanville Pl *KESG* IP5 24 D2
Glanville Rd *HADL* IP7 37 E5
Glastonbury Cl *CHTY* IP2 30 B2
Glebe Cl *RIPW* IP8 20 B2
Glebe End *RIPS/CAP* IP9 41 F1
Glebe Wy *NHMKT* IP6 7 E2
Glemham Dr *IPNE* IP4 24 B4
Glemsford Cl *FX* IP11 44 D4
Glenavon Rd *IPNE* IP4 23 H1
Glencoe Rd *IPNE* IP4 13 G4
Gleneagles Cl *FX* IP11 46 A3
Gleneagles Dr *IPNE* IP4 23 H3
Glenfield Av *FX* IP11 45 G1
Glenhurst Av *IPNE* IP4 13 F5
Gloster Rd *KESG* IP5 26 B1
Gloucester Rd *IPSE* IP3 32 A1
Godbold Cl *KESG* IP5 25 F1
Goddard Rd *IP* IP1 10 C2
Goddard Rd East *IP* IP1 10 D2
Godfrey's Wd *WDBR* IP12 9 G2
Goldcrest Rd *CHTY* IP2 20 C5
Goldsmith Rd *IP* IP1 11 E1
Golf Rd *FX* IP11 46 B4
Gonville Cl *WDBR* IP12 9 E3
Goodwood Cl *IP* IP1 11 H1
Gordon Rd *IPNE* IP4 23 E1
Goring Rd *IPNE* IP4 23 F2
Gorsehayes *CHTY* IP2 21 H5
Gorse Rd *IPSE* IP3 32 B1
Gosford Wy *FX* IP11 46 A3
Gostling Pl *KESG* IP5 15 G5
Gowers Cl *KESG* IP5 25 G1
Gower St *CHTY* IP2 2 E6
Goyfield Av *FX* IP11 45 F3
Grafton Wy *IP* IP1 2 D5
Graham Av *IP* IP1 11 H5
Graham Rd *FX* IP11 45 F2
IP IP1 21 H1
Grange Cl *FX* IP11 45 E2
KESG IP5 15 G5
Grange Ct *WDBR* IP12 9 H2
Grange Farm Av *FX* IP11 44 D3
Grange La *KESG* IP5 15 G5
Grange Rd *FX* IP11 44 D3
IPNE IP4 3 J4
Grantchester Pl *KESG* IP5 24 C1
Grantham Crs *CHTY* IP2 2 A7
Granville Rd *FX* IP11 45 F4
Granville St *IP* IP1 2 B2
Granworth Cl *FRAM/WMKT* IP13 27 A2
Grasmere Av *FX* IP11 46 B3
Grasmere Cl *IPSE* IP3 32 B3
Gray's Orch *KIR/NAC* IP10 42 C4
Great Colman St *IPNE* IP4 2 E3
Great Eastern Sq *FX* IP11 45 G2
Great Fld *FX* IP11 43 C4
Great Gipping St *IP* IP1 2 C4
Great Tufts *RIPS/CAP* IP9 41 F2
Great Whip St *CHTY* IP2 2 E6
Grebe Cl *CHTY* IP2 30 A1
The Green *FRAM/WMKT* IP13 27 A3
HADL IP7 37 E3
Green Crs *KIR/NAC* IP10 35 E3
Greenfinch Av *CHTY* IP2 20 D5
Green La *NHMKT* IP6 13 G1
WDBR IP12 16 B3
Green Man Wy *WDBR* IP12 9 H2
Green Oak Gld *RIPW* IP8 29 H3
The Greens *IPNE* IP4 24 B4
Greenspire Gv *RIPW* IP8 29 F1
Greenways Cl *IP* IP1 11 H5
Greenwich Cl *IPSE* IP3 31 G1
Greenwich Rd *IPSE* IP3 31 F1
Greyfriars *IP* IP1 2 C4
WDBR IP12 8 D4
Grey Friars Rd *IP* IP1 2 D5
Griffin Ct *CHTY* * IP2 22 B5
Grimwade St *IPNE* IP4 3 G5
The Grindle *RIPW* IP8 19 H1
Grinstead Gdns *NHMKT* IP6 4 D5
Grinstead Hl *NHMKT* IP6 4 D5
The Grove *IP* IP1 12 A3
KESG IP5 16 A5
WDBR IP12 9 H3
Grosvenor Cl *IPNE* IP4 12 C5
Grove Gdns *WDBR* IP12 9 E3
Grove Hl *RIPW* IP8 29 G4
Grove La *IPNE* IP4 3 J4
Grove Rd *FRAM/WMKT* IP13 9 E2
FX IP11 45 G1
Grundisburgh Rd
FRAM/WMKT IP13 27 D4
WDBR IP12 9 E3
Gulpher Rd *FX* IP11 45 E1
Gurdon Rd *FRAM/WMKT* IP13 27 B3
Guston Gdns *KIR/NAC* IP10 42 C4
Guthrum Rd *HADL* IP7 36 D3
Gwendoline Rd *IPNE* IP4 24 A4
Gymnasium St *IP* IP1 2 B2

H

Hackney Rd *WDBR* IP12 9 H2
Hadleigh Rd *RIPW* IP8 20 C4
Hale Cl *CHTY* IP2 29 H1
Halesowen Cl *CHTY* IP2 30 B3
Half Moon La *FRAM/WMKT* IP13 27 B3
Halford Ct *RIPW* IP8 29 G1
Halifax Rd *CHTY* IP2 30 D1
Hall Farm Rd *WDBR* IP12 9 H1
Hall Fld *FX* IP11 44 D2
Halliwell Rd *IPNE* IP4 23 F2
Hall La *NHMKT* IP6 7 G4
Hall Pond Wy *FX* IP11 44 D2
Hall Rd *KESG* IP5 15 G3
KIR/NAC IP10 25 G4
Halton Crs *IPSE* IP3 32 C2
Hamblin Rd *WDBR* IP12 9 G3
Hamilton Gdns *FX* IP11 45 G4
Hamilton Rd *FX* IP11 45 G3
IPSE IP3 23 F5
Hamilton St *FX* IP11 45 E2
Hampton Rd *IP* IP1 21 F1
Handford Cut *IP* IP1 2 A3
Handford Rd *IP* IP1 2 A3
Hardwick Cl *IPNE* IP4 24 A3
Hardy Crs *IP* IP1 11 F1
Harebell Rd *CHTY* IP2 21 F4
Hargrave Av *NHMKT* IP6 4 C5
Harrier Cl *IPSE* IP3 32 B2
Harrison Gv *KESG* IP5 15 E5
Harrow Cl *IPNE* IP4 23 E3
Hartley St *CHTY* IP2 22 A5
Harvest Ct *FX* * IP11 45 H3
Harvesters Wy *KESG* IP5 25 H2
Hasketon Rd *FRAM/WMKT* IP13 9 E2
FRAM/WMKT IP13 27 C2
Haskins Wk *KESG* IP5 25 G1
Haslemere Dr *IPNE* IP4 3 J1
Hatfield Rd *IPSE* IP3 23 E4
Haughgate Cl *WDBR* IP12 9 F2
Haugh La *WDBR* IP12 9 F1
Haughley Dr *IPNE* IP4 24 B2
Hauliers Rd *FX* IP11 44 D5
Haven Cl *FX* IP11 44 D3
Haven Ex *FX* * IP11 44 D5
The Havens *KIR/NAC* IP10 33 E4
Hawbridge *RIPS/CAP* IP9 41 E1
Hawes St *CHTY* IP2 22 B5
Hawke Rd *IPSE* IP3 31 G2
Hawker Dr *KESG* IP5 16 B5
Hawkes La *FX* IP11 44 D1
Hawks Mill St *NHMKT* IP6 4 C3
Hawthorn Dr *CHTY* IP2 29 H1
Hawthorn Pl *WDBR* IP12 9 E2
Hayhill Rd *IPNE* IP4 3 H1
Hayman Rd *IPSE* IP3 31 H2
Haywards Flds *KESG* IP5 15 F5
Hazelcroft Rd *IP* IP1 11 H3
Hazel Dr *IPSE* IP3 33 E2
Hazel Ri *NHMKT* IP6 7 E4
Hazlitt Rd *IP* IP1 11 G2
Headingham Cl *CHTY* IP2 30 C1
Heath Ct *FX* IP11 43 B2
Heath Rd *KIR/NAC* IP10 26 D3
Heather Av *IPSE* IP3 23 G5
Heather Cl *KIR/NAC* IP10 25 H3
Heathercroft Rd *IP* IP1 11 G1
Heatherhayes *CHTY* IP2 21 H5

Heathfield *KESG* IP5 25 H2
Heathfield Ms *KIR/NAC* IP10 25 H3
Heathfields *FX* IP11 43 A1
Heathgate Piece *FX* IP11 43 C4
Heathlands Pk *IPNE* IP4 24 A4
Heath La *IPNE* IP4 23 G3
Heath Rd *IPNE* IP4 23 G2
Heath Vw *KESG* IP5 24 C2
Helena Rd *IPSE* IP3 3 H7
Helston Cl *KESG* IP5 24 D2
Henderson Cl *RIPW* IP8 10 A4
Hengrave Cl *CHTY* IP2 30 C1
Henley Av *IP* IP1 11 H2
Henley Rd *IP* IP1 11 H1
IP IP1 12 A4
Henniker Rd *IP* IP1 10 D5
Henry Rd *IPSE* IP3 32 B2
Henslow Rd *IPNE* IP4 23 F3
Henstead Gdns *IPSE* IP3 32 A1
Herbert Rd *KESG* IP5 15 G5
Heron Rd *CHTY* IP2 21 E5
Hervey St *IPNE* IP4 3 G1
Heywood Cl *CHTY* IP2 29 H2
Hibbard Rd *RIPW* IP8 10 C3
Higgins Pl *KESG* * IP5 26 A1
High Beach *FX* IP11 46 A5
Highfield Ap *IP* IP1 11 F4
Highfield Dr *NHMKT* IP6 7 F3
Highfield Rd *FX* IP11 45 G3
IP IP1 11 E3
High Hall Cl *FX* IP11 43 A2
Highlands Cl *NHMKT* IP6 4 B3
Highlands Rd *HADL* IP7 36 D4
High Rd *FX* IP11 43 B3
High Rd East *FX* IP11 45 H2
High Rd West *FX* IP11 45 F1
High Row Fld *FX* IP11 46 A4
High St *FX* IP11 45 E1
HADL IP7 36 D3
IP IP1 2 D2
NHMKT IP6 4 C3
RIPW IP8 20 A2
High View Rd *IP* IP1 10 D5
Hildabrook Cl *CHTY* IP2 30 A2
Hillary Cl *IPNE* IP4 23 E3
Hillcrest Ap *RIPW* IP8 10 B3
Hill Farm Rd *NHMKT* IP6 14 D1
Hill House La *NHMKT* IP6 4 B3
Hill House Rd *IPNE* IP4 3 J5
Hillside Crs *IPSE* IP3 23 F5
Hill View Ter *WDBR* * IP12 9 G3
Hilly Flds *WDBR* IP12 9 E5
Hilton Rd *IPSE* IP3 32 C2
KESG IP5 16 C5
Hines Rd *IPSE* IP3 23 E4
Hintesham Cl *IPNE* IP4 24 B3
Hintlesham Dr *FX* IP11 44 D2
Histon Cl *KESG* IP5 24 B1
Hockney Gdns *IPSE* IP3 32 A3
Hodgkinson Rd *FX* IP11 44 C4
Hogarth Rd *IPSE* IP3 31 H2
Hogarth Sq *IPSE* IP3 31 H2
Holbecks La *HADL* IP7 36 C5
Holbrook Crs *FX* IP11 44 D3
Holbrook Rd *IPSE* IP3 31 G2
Holcombe Crs *CHTY* IP2 29 H1
Holfen Cl *WDBR* IP12 16 C3
Holkham Cl *IPNE* IP4 24 B3
Holland Rd *FX* IP11 45 F4
IPNE IP4 22 D2
Hollow Rd *RIPW* IP8 28 B3
Holly Blue Cl *RIPW* IP8 30 A3
Hollybush Dr *FX* IP11 46 B2
Hollycroft Cl *IP* IP1 11 G2
Holly End *KESG* IP5 25 H2
Holly La *KESG* IP5 14 A3
RIPW IP8 29 G3
Holly Rd *IP* IP1 21 H1
KESG IP5 24 B1
Holm Ct *KESG* * IP5 15 F5
Holt's La *NHMKT* IP6 5 E2
Holyrood Cl *CHTY* IP2 30 B2
Holywells Cl *IPSE* IP3 3 J7
Holy Wells Rd *IPSE* IP3 22 C5
Homefield *RIPS/CAP* IP9 41 F2
Homer Cl *IP* IP1 11 F1
Honeysuckle Gdns *CHTY* IP2 21 E4
Hood Dr *NHMKT* IP6 6 B2
Hood Rd *IPSE* IP3 31 G2
Hook La *HADL* IP7 37 F5
Hope Crs *WDBR* IP12 9 G2
Horsham Av *IPSE* IP3 23 H5
Hossack Rd *IPSE* IP3 32 A3
Houghton Pl *IPNE* IP4 24 B3
Horseman Ct *KESG* IP5 26 B1
Howard St *IPNE* IP4 23 F1
Howards Wy *KESG* IP5 15 G5
Howe Av *IPSE* IP3 23 G5
Howlett Cl *KESG* IP5 25 G1
Humber Doucy La *IPNE* IP4 13 E3
Hunters Ride *KESG* IP5 26 B1
Hunter Rd *IPSE* IP3 32 C3
Hunters End *FX* IP11 43 C5
Hurdle Makers Hl *RIPW* IP8 19 F4
Hurricane Pl *IPSE* IP3 32 C2
Hurstlea Rd *NHMKT* IP6 4 B3
Hutland Rd *IPNE* IP4 22 D1
Hyntle Cl *CHTY* IP2 21 E3

I

Ickworth Ct *FX* IP11 44 C4
Ickworth Crs *IPNE* IP4 24 B3
Inkerman Cl *HADL* IP7 36 D3
Inkerman Ter *HADL* IP7 36 D3
Inverness Rd *IPNE* IP4 13 E3
Ipswich Rd *FRAM/WMKT* IP13 27 A4
HADL IP7 37 F1
KIR/NAC IP10 33 F5
NHMKT IP6 4 D4
WDBR IP12 8 D5
Ireland Rd *IPSE* IP3 31 H2
Iris Cl *CHTY* IP2 21 F3
Irlam Rd *CHTY* IP2 29 H1
Ivry St *IP* IP1 21 H1

J

Jack's Green Rd *NHMKT* IP6 4 C1
Jackson Ct *KESG* * IP5 26 A1
Jackson Wy *NHMKT* IP6 4 C4
Jacob Wy *WDBR* IP12 9 G3
Jacqueline Cl *FRAM/WMKT* IP13 27 B3
James Boden Cl *FX* * IP11 45 E2
Janebrook Rd *CHTY* IP2 30 A1
Jasmine Cl *CHTY* IP2 21 F5
FX IP11 43 B2
Jeavons La *KESG* IP5 25 G1
Jefferies Rd *IPNE* IP4 3 H3
Jenners Cl *WDBR* IP12 9 H2
Jermyns Cl *RIPS/CAP* IP9 41 F1
Jewell Vw *KESG* IP5 25 F1
Johnson Cl *CHTY* IP2 22 A5
John Swain Cl *NHMKT* IP6 4 B3
Jordan Cl *NHMKT* IP6 4 D2
Jordayn Cl *HADL* IP7 37 E4
The Josselyns *FX* IP11 43 C4
Jubilee Cl *FX* IP11 43 B2
NHMKT IP6 7 E3
June Av *IP* IP1 11 H3
Jupiter Rd *IPNE* IP4 23 F1

K

Karen Cl *IP* IP1 11 H4
Keats Crs *IP* IP1 11 F2
Keeper's La *FX* IP11 43 A5
Kelly Rd *CHTY* IP2 21 E3
Kelvedon Dr *IPNE* IP4 24 B3
Kelvin Rd *IP* IP1 11 F4
Kemball St *IPNE* IP4 23 E3
The Kempsters *FX* IP11 43 D5
Kempton Cl *IP* IP1 11 G2
Kempton Rd *IP* IP1 11 G2
Kemsley Rd *FX* IP11 45 F2
Kennedy Cl *IPNE* IP4 23 E2
Kennels Rd *KIR/NAC* IP10 34 C1
Kenney Cl *RIPW* IP8 18 D2
Kensington Rd *IP* IP1 11 G5
Kentford Rd *FX* IP11 44 C3
Kentwell Cl *IPNE* IP4 24 B4
Kenyon St *CHTY* IP2 2 E7
Kerry Av *IP* IP1 10 D4
Kersey Rd *FX* IP11 44 D4
Kesteven Rd *CHTY* IP2 2 A7
Kestrel Rd *CHTY* IP2 20 D5
Keswick Cl *FX* IP11 46 A3
Kettlebaston Wy *IP* IP1 12 B4
Kettle La *NHMKT* IP6 5 F4
Key St *IPSE* IP3 3 F5
Keytes Wy *NHMKT* IP6 6 B2
Khartoum Rd *IPNE* IP4 22 D1
Kildare Av *IP* IP1 10 D3
Kiln Fld *FX* IP11 44 D2
King Edward Rd *IPSE* IP3 23 F5
Kingfisher Av *CHTY* IP2 20 D5
Kingfisher Dr *NHMKT* IP6 6 B2
Kings Av *IPNE* IP4 3 H4
Kingsbury Rd *FX* IP11 43 C5
Kingsfield Av *IP* IP1 12 B4
Kings Fleet Rd *FX* IP11 45 E4
Kingsgate Dr *IPNE* IP4 12 D5
Kingsley Cl *IP* IP1 11 G2
Kingston Farm Rd *WDBR* IP12 9 F5
Kingston Rd *IP* IP1 11 F5
WDBR IP12 9 G4
King St *FX* IP11 45 E2
IP IP1 2 D3
King's Wy *IPSE* IP3 32 B1
Kingsway *WDBR* IP12 9 H3
King William St *NHMKT* IP6 4 C3
Kinross Rd *IPNE* IP4 13 F4
Kipling Rd *IP* IP1 11 F2
Kirby Cl *IPNE* IP4 23 E1
Kirby St *IPNE* IP4 23 E1
Kirkham Cl *CHTY* IP2 30 C1
Kirton Rd *KIR/NAC* IP10 42 B5
Kitchener Rd *IP* IP1 11 F5
Kittiwake Cl *CHTY* IP2 21 E5
Knights Cl *FX* IP11 46 B3
Knightsdale Rd *IP* IP1 11 G4
Knights La *KESG* IP5 25 F1
Knutsford Cl *RIPW* IP8 29 G2

L

Laburnum Cl *IPSE* IP3 33 E1
RIPW IP8 29 G1
Laburnum Gdns *KESG* IP5 14 A4
Lacey St *IPNE* IP4 3 H2
Lacon Rd *RIPW* IP8 10 A3
Lady La *HADL* IP7 37 E2
IP IP1 2 C3
Lady Margaret Gdns *WDBR* IP12 8 D4
Ladywood Rd *IPNE* IP4 23 G1
Lagonda Drive *IP* IP1 10 C3
Lakeside Rd *CHTY* IP2 30 A1
Lamberts La *KESG* IP5 13 G3
Lambeth Cl *IP* IP1 11 F5
Lambourne Rd *IP* IP1 11 H1
Lanark Rd *IPNE* IP4 13 F4
Lancaster Dr *KESG* IP5 26 B2
Lancaster Rd *IPNE* IP4 3 H3
Lancaster Wy *NHMKT* IP6 7 E3
The Lancers *WDBR* IP12 8 D5
Lancing Av *IPNE* IP4 13 E5
Landguard Rd *FX* IP11 47 C2
Landseer Cl *IPSE* IP3 32 A2
Landseer Rd *IPSE* IP3 31 G1
Lanercost Wy *CHTY* IP2 30 C2
Langdale Cl *FX* IP11 46 B3
Langer Rd *FX* IP11 45 E5
Langley Av *FX* IP11 45 E3
Langley Cl *FX* IP11 45 E2
Langstons *FX* IP11 43 D4
Lansdowne Rd *FX* IP11 45 H1
IPNE IP4 23 E3
Lapwing Rd *CHTY* IP2 20 D5
Larchcroft Cl *IP* IP1 11 H3
Larchcroft Rd *IP* IP1 11 H3
Larchwood Cl *CHTY* IP2 20 C3
Largent Gv *KESG* IP5 15 G5
Lark Rise *KESG* IP5 26 A1
Larkhill Ri *IPNE* IP4 24 A3
Larkhill Wy *FX* IP11 44 D2
Larkspur Rd *CHTY* IP2 21 F5
Larksway *FX* IP11 44 D4
Lattice Av *IPNE* IP4 23 G2
Lattinford Br *RIPS/CAP* * IP9 40 C4
Laud's Cl *FX* IP11 43 B4
Laurel Av *KESG* IP5 24 C1
Laurel Cottages *FX* * IP11 46 A1
Laurel Dr *NHMKT* IP6 6 C2
Laurelhayes *CHTY* IP2 21 G5
Laurel Wy *NHMKT* IP6 7 E4
Lavender Hl *CHTY* IP2 21 F4
Lavenham Rd *CHTY* IP2 21 E3
The Lawns *IPNE* IP4 13 G5
Lawn Wy *FX* IP11 45 E2
Layham Rd *HADL* IP7 36 D5
Leeks Hl *WDBR* IP12 9 G1
Lee Rd *IPSE* IP3 22 D5
Leeward Ct *FX* * IP11 45 G2
Leggatt Dr *RIPW* IP8 10 A3
Leicester Cl *CHTY* IP2 30 B2
Leighton Rd *IPSE* IP3 32 A3
Leighton Sq *IPSE* IP3 32 A3
Lely Rd *IPSE* IP3 31 H3
Leopold Gdns *IPNE* IP4 13 E5
Leopold Rd *FX* IP11 45 G3
IPNE IP4 23 E1
Leslie Rd *IPSE* IP3 32 C2
Letton Cl *RIPS/CAP* IP9 41 E2
Levington La *KIR/NAC* IP10 35 E3
Levington Rd *FX* IP11 47 C1
IPSE IP3 23 E4
KIR/NAC IP10 39 E2
Lewes Cl *IPSE* IP3 24 A5
Lidgate Ct *FX* IP11 44 C3
Lilac Wk *NHMKT* IP6 4 C5
Limecroft Cl *IP* IP1 11 G2
Limekiln Cl *NHMKT* IP6 7 E4
Lime Kiln Quay Rd *WDBR* IP12 9
Limerick Cl *IP* IP1 11
The Limes *KESG* IP5 13
Limes Av *RIPW* IP8 10
Limetree Cl *NHMKT* IP6 4
Lincoln Cl *IP* IP1 11
Lincoln Gdns *NHMKT* IP6 7
Lincoln Ter *FX* IP11 45
Lindbergh Rd *IPSE* IP3 32
Lindisfarne Cl *CHTY* IP2 30
Lindsey Rd *IPNE* IP4 23
Lingfield Rd *IP* IP1 11
Lingside *KESG* IP5 25
The Link *RIPS/CAP* IP9 41
Link La *RIPS/CAP* IP9 41
Link Rd *RIPS/CAP* IP9 41
Links Av *FX* IP11 45
Linksfield *KESG* IP5 24
Linksfield Gdns *KESG* IP5 24
Linnet Rd *CHTY* IP2 20
Lion La *NHMKT* IP6 4
Lion St *IP* IP1 2
Lister Rd *HADL* IP7 37
IP IP1 11
Little Croft St *CHTY* IP2 22
Little Gipping St *IP* IP1 2
Little Gv *RIPS/CAP* IP9 41
Little Gulls *RIPS/CAP* IP9 40
Little St John's St *WDBR* IP12 9
Little's Crs *CHTY* IP2 2
Little Tufts *RIPS/CAP* IP9 41
Little Whip St *CHTY* IP2 2
The Lloyds *KESG* IP5 25
Lloyds Av *IP* IP1 2
Locarno Rd *IPSE* IP3 23
Lockwood Cl *WDBR* IP12 9
Lodge Farm Dr *FX* IP11 46
Lodge La *NHMKT* IP6 6
London Rd *CHTY* IP2 20
RIPS/CAP IP9 41
RIPW IP8 28
Lone Barn Ct *IP* IP1 10
Long Bessels *HADL* IP7 36
Longcroft *FX* IP11 45
Long Fld *FX* IP11 44
Longfield Rd *RIPS/CAP* IP9 41
Long Perry *RIPS/CAP* IP9 41
Long St *IPNE* IP4 3
Lonsdale Cl *IPNE* IP4 22
Looe Rd *FX* IP11 46
Loraine Wy *RIPW* IP8 10
Lotus Cl *IP* IP1 10
Lovetofts Dr *IP* IP1 10
Lower Barn Rd *RIPW* IP8 28
Lower Brook St *IPNE* IP4 2
Lower Crs *NHMKT* IP6 6
Lower Dales View Rd *IP* IP1 11
Lower Orwell St *IPNE* IP4 3
Lower Rd *FRAM/WMKT* IP13 27
Lower St *RIPW* IP8 20
Lowry Gdns *IPSE* IP3 32
Ludbrook Cl *NHMKT* IP6 4
Ludlow Cl *IP* IP1 11
Luff Meadow *NHMKT* IP6 4
Lugano Av *KESG* IP5 16
Lulworth Av *IPSE* IP3 23
Lummis V *KESG* IP5 25
Lupin Rd *CHTY* IP2 21
Lupin Wy *NHMKT* IP6 4
Luther Rd *CHTY* IP2 2
Lyndhurst Av *IPNE* IP4 23
Lynwood Av *FX* IP11 45
Lysander Dr *IPSE* IP3 32

M

Macaulay Rd *IP* IP1 11
Mackenzie Dr *KESG* IP5 14
Magdalen Dr *WDBR* IP12 8
Magdalene Cl *CHTY* IP2 30
Magdalen Rd *HADL* IP7 36
Magingley Crs *KESG* IP5 24
Magpie Cl *RIPW* IP8 29
Maidenhall Ap *CHTY* IP2 30
Maidstone Rd *FX* IP11 45
Main Rd *IPNE* IP4 13
KESG IP5 14
KIR/NAC IP10 34
WDBR IP12 16
WDBR IP12 16
Maitland Rd *NHMKT* IP6 4
Mallard Wy *CHTY* IP2 30
Mallowhayes Cl *CHTY* IP2 21
Malmesbury Cl *CHTY* IP2 30
Malting Ter *CHTY* * IP2 3
Malvern Cl *IPSE* IP3 23
KESG IP5 24
Manchester Rd *CHTY* IP2 29

ndy Cl IPNE IP4 23 E2
nnall Wk KESG IP5 15 G5
nning Rd FX IP11 45 F5
nnington Cl IPNE IP4 24 B3
nor Rd FRAM/WMKT IP13 8 D2
X IP11 43 B4
X IP11 47 C1
PNE IP4 12 B5
ESG IP5 16 A5
nor Ter FX IP11 47 C2
nsfield Av IP IP1 11 F3
nwick Rd FX IP11 45 E5
ple Cl CHTY IP2 21 G5
ple Gv NHMKT IP6 6 D1
e Maples KESG IP5 14 A5
rbled White Dr RIPW IP8 30 A3
rcus Rd FX IP11 46 B4
rgaret St FX IP11 45 E2
rgate Rd IPSE IP3 23 F5
rgery Girling House FX * IP11 46 A3
rigold Av CHTY IP2 21 E5
rina Gdns FX IP11 45 E5
rket Hl WDBR IP12 9 F3
rket Pl HADL IP7 36 D4
rket Rd IP IP1 2 C4
rlborough Rd IPNE IP4 22 D3
rlow Rd IP IP1 10 D4
rshall Cl KESG IP5 15 E5
rtello La FX IP11 46 B4
rtinet Gn IPSE IP3 32 B2
rtin Rd CHTY IP2 2 D7
rtinsyde KESG IP5 16 B5
rtlesham Rd
FRAM/WMKT IP13 15 H2
ryon Rd IPSE IP3 32 B3
son Ct NHMKT IP6 6 D3
sons Cl IPNE IP4 22 D2
sterson Gv KESG IP5 25 E2
ther Wy CHTY IP2 3 F7
tlock Cl RIPW IP8 29 G1
tson Rd IP IP1 11 F5
udslay Rd IP IP1 10 C3
ybury Rd IPSE IP3 32 B2
ybush La FX IP11 46 A4
ycroft Cl IP IP1 11 G1
yfield La KESG IP5 26 A2
yfield Rd IPNE IP4 23 G1
yfields KESG IP5 26 A2
y Rd IPSE IP3 32 C1
eadow Cl FX IP11 43 B2
eadowlands KIR/NAC IP10 42 B4
eadowside Gdns IPNE IP4 14 A5
eadows Wy HADL IP7 36 D3
eadowvale Cl IPNE IP4 22 D1
eadow Vw NHMKT IP6 4 B3
edway Rd IPSE IP3 31 H1
eeting La FRAM/WMKT IP13 27 A3
elbourne Rd IPNE IP4 23 H1
elford Cl IPNE IP4 24 B3
elford Wy FX IP11 44 C4
ellis Ct FX IP11 44 D2
elplash Cl IPSE IP3 24 A4
elplash Rd IPSE IP3 24 A4
elrose Gdns IPNE IP4 13 F5
elton Grange Rd WDBR IP12 9 G2
elton Hl WDBR IP12 9 H3
elton Meadow Rd WDBR IP12 9 G2
elton Rd WDBR IP12 9 H2
elville Rd IPNE IP4 3 K4
endip Dr KESG IP5 24 B2
eredith Rd IP IP1 11 E3
ere Gdns IPNE IP4 24 B4
eriton Ri HADL IP7 37 F5
erlin Rd CHTY IP2 20 C5
errion Cl RIPW IP8 29 G1
ersey Rd IPSE IP3 22 D5
ichigan Cl KESG IP5 24 D1
ickfield Ms FX * IP11 44 D2
icklegate Rd FX IP11 45 E5
iddleton Cl CHTY IP2 29 H1
iddleton Rd NHMKT IP6 7 E3
ilano Av KESG IP5 16 C5
ilden Rd CHTY IP2 21 E3
ildmay Rd IPSE IP3 32 A2
ill Cl FX IP11 43 A2
FX IP11 44 D3
RIPS/CAP IP9 40 C2
illers Ct NHMKT IP6 6 D3
ill Fld RIPW IP8 10 B3
illfield Gdns IPNE IP4 23 E1
ill Hl FRAM/WMKT IP13 27 B2
RIPS/CAP IP9 40 C2
ill La FRAM/WMKT IP13 8 A1
FX IP11 43 A2
FX IP11 45 F3
NHMKT IP6 6 B2
RIPW IP8 10 B4
RIPW IP8 28 D2
WDBR IP12 9 G3
ill Piece KIR/NAC IP10 33 H5
Mill Rd IPSE IP3 33 F2
The Mills IPNE IP4 14 A5
Mill View Cl WDBR IP12 9 E3
Milner St IPNE IP4 3 H4
Milnrow RIPW IP8 29 G1
Milton St IPNE IP4 23 E1
Mistley Wy WDBR IP12 9 F2
Mitford Cl IP IP1 11 G1
Mitre Wy IPSE IP3 3 J6
Moat Farm Cl IPNE IP4 12 D5
Moffat Av IPNE IP4 13 F4
Monks Cl FX IP11 46 B3
Monks Ga RIPW IP8 20 A2
Monmouth Cl CHTY IP2 30 D2
Montague Rd FX IP11 45 G3
Montana Rd KESG IP5 24 C1
Montgomery Rd CHTY IP2 30 D2
Monton Ri CHTY IP2 29 H1
Monument Farm Rd
KIR/NAC IP10 25 E4
Moore Rd IP IP1 11 F2
Moorfield Cl KESG IP5 25 E1
Moorfield Rd WDBR IP12 9 E3
Moor's Wy WDBR IP12 9 E3
Morgan Ct NHMKT IP6 7 E4
Morgan Dr IP IP1 10 C4
Morland Rd IPSE IP3 32 A3
Morley Av WDBR IP12 9 F4
Mornington Av IP IP1 11 F4
Morris Wy NHMKT IP6 4 C4
Moss La NHMKT IP6 12 D1
Mottram Cl RIPW IP8 29 G1
Mountbatten Ct IP IP1 2 A1
Mount Dr IPSE IP3 33 F2
Mowlands RIPS/CAP IP9 41 F2
Mulberry Gdns NHMKT IP6 6 C2
Mumford Rd IP IP1 11 E5
Munnings Cl IPSE IP3 32 B3
Muriel Cl HADL IP7 37 E3
Murray Rd IPSE IP3 23 E5
Murrills Rd IPSE IP3 33 F2
Museum St IP IP1 2 D3
Mussiden Pl WDBR * IP12 9 F3
Myrtle Rd IPSE IP3 3 J7

N

Nacton Crs IPSE IP3 32 B1
Nacton Rd FX IP11 47 C1
IPSE IP3 3 K6
IPSE IP3 32 D3
Nansen Rd IPSE IP3 32 B1
Naunton Rd WDBR IP12 9 E3
Navarre St IP IP1 2 E2
Naverne Meadow WDBR IP12 9 G3
Nayland Rd FX IP11 44 C4
Neale St IP IP1 2 E2
Neath Dr CHTY IP2 30 C2
Nelson Rd IPNE IP4 23 E1
Nelson Wy WDBR IP12 9 F1
Neptune Quay IPSE * IP3 3 G5
Neptune Sq IPSE IP3 3 G5
Netley Cl CHTY IP2 30 B3
Newark Cl CHTY IP2 30 B2
Newbourne Gdns FX IP11 44 D4
Newbourne Rd KIR/NAC IP10 26 B4
Newbury Rd IPNE IP4 23 F3
Newby Dr IPNE IP4 24 B3
New Cardinal St IP IP1 2 C5
New Cut HADL IP7 37 E3
Newell Ri NHMKT IP6 7 E4
Newhaven Wy HADL IP7 37 E2
Newnham Av WDBR IP12 8 D4
Newnham Ct CHTY IP2 30 A2
Newquay Cl KESG IP5 24 B2
New Rd FX IP11 43 C5
Newry Av FX IP11 45 F3
Newson St IP IP1 2 C1
New St WDBR IP12 9 G3
Newton Rd IPSE IP3 23 E4
Newton St IPNE IP4 3 G3
New Wy CHTY IP2 21 F2
Nicholas Rd FX IP11 44 C3
Nightingale Rd IPSE IP3 32 A3
Nightingale Sq IPSE IP3 32 A3
Nine Acres CHTY IP2 20 D2
Norbury Rd IPNE IP4 23 F1
Norfolk Rd IPNE IP4 3 G2
Norman Cl FX IP11 46 B3
WDBR IP12 9 G2
Norman Crs IPSE IP3 32 A1
North Cl IPNE IP4 12 C5
Northgate St IP IP1 2 E3
North Hl WDBR IP12 9 F2
North Hill Gdns IPNE IP4 3 J2
North Hill Rd IPNE IP4 3 J2
North Lawn IPNE IP4 13 F5
North Quay FX * IP11 47 A1
Norwich Rd IP IP1 2 A1
Nottidge Rd IPNE IP4 3 J3
Nunn Cl WDBR IP12 16 B3
Nursery Wk FX IP11 45 F3

O

Oak Cl FX IP11 45 E3
Oakdene KIR/NAC IP10 42 B4
Oakfield Rd RIPW IP8 28 D5
Oak Gv RIPW IP8 20 A2
Oak Hill La CHTY IP2 21 H5
The Oaks KESG IP5 25 H2
Oaksmere Gdns CHTY IP2 30 C1
Oakstead Cl IPNE IP4 22 D2
Oban St IP IP1 2 B1
Old Barrack Rd WDBR IP12 8 D5
Old Cattle Market IPNE IP4 2 E4
Oldfield Rd RIPW IP8 29 F2
Old Foundry Rd IPNE IP4 3 F3
Old Ipswich Rd NHMKT IP6 7 E4
Old Kirton Rd FX IP11 43 A2
Old London Rd RIPS/CAP IP9 40 D4
Old Paper Mill La NHMKT IP6 7 E5
Old Rectory Cl NHMKT IP6 7 E2
The Old St RIPS/CAP IP9 41 F2
Olympus Cl IP IP1 10 C3
Onehouse La IP IP1 11 H4
Opal Av IP IP1 10 D4
Orchard Cl WDBR IP12 9 G1
Orchard End FRAM/WMKT IP13 27 B3
Orchard Ga CHTY IP2 20 C3
NHMKT IP6 4 B3
Orchard Gv KESG IP5 24 C1
NHMKT IP6 7 E5
Orchard Rd RIPW IP8 10 A3
Orchard Rw FX * IP11 45 E2
Orchard St IPNE IP4 3 G3
Orchid Cl CHTY IP2 21 E4
Orchid Wy NHMKT IP6 4 C5
Oregon Rd KESG IP5 24 C2
Orford Rd FX IP11 47 C1
Orford St IP IP1 2 B1
Orkney Rd IPNE IP4 13 E4
Orwell Gdns CHTY * IP2 21 G5
Orwell Pl IPNE IP4 3 F4
Orwell Rd FX IP11 45 G4
IPSE IP3 23 E4
Osborne Rd IPSE IP3 23 E4
Osier Cl WDBR IP12 9 H2
Otley Ct FX IP11 44 D2
Oulton Rd IPSE IP3 31 G1
Oxford Dr WDBR IP12 8 D5
Oxford Rd IPNE IP4 3 H4
KESG IP5 24 C1

P

Packard Av IPSE IP3 32 B1
Packard Pl RIPW IP8 10 B3
The Paddocks KESG IP5 16 A5
Padstow Rd KESG IP5 24 C2
Page Gdns KESG IP5 15 G5
Paget Cl NHMKT IP6 4 B3
Paget Rd IP IP1 21 H1
Palmcroft Cl IP IP1 11 G2
Palmcroft Rd IP IP1 11 G2
Palmerston Rd IPNE IP4 3 H3
Parade Rd IPNE IP4 3 K1
Pardoe Pl IPNE IP4 24 A3
Park Av FX IP11 45 H2
Park Cl KESG IP5 16 A5
Parker Av FX IP11 44 B4
Parkers Pl KESG IP5 16 A5
Parkeston Rd FX IP11 44 D3
Park Farm Cottages FX * IP11 46 A2
Park La KIR/NAC IP10 42 B2
Park North IP IP1 12 B5
Park Rd FRAM/WMKT IP13 27 A4
IP IP1 12 A5
NHMKT IP6 4 C3
Park View Rd IP IP1 11 G4
Parliament Rd IPNE IP4 23 F3
Parnell Cl IP IP1 11 F2
Parnell Rd IP IP1 11 F2
Parnham Pl IPNE IP4 24 B3
Parsonage Cl FX IP11 44 D3
Partridge Rd CHTY IP2 20 D5
The Pastures IPNE IP4 24 B3
Patteson Rd IPSE IP3 3 H7
Pauline St CHTY IP2 22 A5
Paul's Rd CHTY IP2 21 F3
Peacock St KESG IP5 25 G1
Pearce Rd IPSE IP3 23 E3
Pearcroft Rd IP IP1 11 H2
Pearl Rd IP IP1 10 C5
Pearse Wy IPSE IP3 33 E2
Pearson Rd IPNE IP4 23 G3
Pearsons Wy RIPW IP8 28 D2
Peel St IP IP1 2 D2
Peel Yd KESG IP5 16 A5
Peewit Ct FX * IP11 44 D4
Peewit Hl FX IP11 44 D5
Peewit Rd CHTY IP2 20 C5
Pelican Cl CHTY IP2 21 E5
Pembroke Av WDBR IP12 9 E4
Pembroke Cl CHTY IP2 21 H5
Pendleton Rd CHTY IP2 29 H2
Penfold Rd FX IP11 45 G3
Penn Cl RIPS/CAP IP9 41 F1
Penny La IPSE IP3 33 F2
Penny Meadow RIPS/CAP IP9 41 E2
Pennyroyal Gdns CHTY IP2 21 E4
Penryn Rd KESG IP5 24 B1
Penshurst Rd IPSE IP3 23 H4
Penzance Rd KESG IP5 24 C2
Peppercorn Wy CHTY IP2 22 A5
Perkins Wy IPSE IP3 31 H2
Pesthouse La NHMKT IP6 6 C1
Peterhouse Cl CHTY IP2 30 A1
Peterhouse Crs WDBR IP12 8 D4
Peter's Gv RIPS/CAP IP9 41 E2
Pheasant Ri RIPW IP8 28 D3
Pheasant Rd CHTY IP2 21 E5
Philip Av FX IP11 44 D4
Philip Rd CHTY IP2 2 D7
Phillipps Rd NHMKT IP6 7 E3
Phillips Crs NHMKT IP6 4 D4
Phoenix Rd IPNE IP4 23 E1
Picketts Rd FX IP11 46 A4
Pickwick Rd CHTY IP2 21 E2
Picton Av IP IP1 12 B4
Pier Rd FX IP11 47 A2
Pigeon's La RIPW IP8 28 B1
The Pightle NHMKT IP6 4 C3
RIPS/CAP IP9 41 F1
Pimpernel Rd CHTY IP2 21 F5
Pine Av IP IP1 11 H4
Pine Bank KESG IP5 25 H2
Pinecroft Rd IP IP1 11 G3
Pinecroft Wy NHMKT IP6 4 D4
Pine Gv FRAM/WMKT IP13 27 B4
The Pines FX IP11 46 C3
Pinetree Cl KESG IP5 24 B1
Pine View Rd IP IP1 11 G5
Pinewood WDBR IP12 9 E5
Pin Mill Cl RIPW IP8 29 G2
Pinners La FRAM/WMKT IP13 8 B1
Pintail Cl CHTY IP2 30 A1
Pitcairn Rd IP IP1 11 E5
Platten Cl NHMKT IP6 4 B3
Platters Cl IPSE IP3 32 A4
Platters Rd FX IP11 45 E5
Playfield Rd RIPS/CAP IP9 41 F2
Playford La KESG IP5 14 A4
Playford Rd IPNE IP4 23 H1
Pleasant Rw IPNE IP4 3 F5
Plough Rd RIPS/CAP IP9 40 D2
Plough St IPSE IP3 3 J6
Plover Rd CHTY IP2 30 A1
Plummers Dell NHMKT IP6 6 C2
Plymouth Rd FX IP11 45 F1
Pond Cl FX IP11 44 D2
Pond Hall Rd HADL IP7 37 G5
Poole Cl IPSE IP3 23 H5
Poplar Cl NHMKT IP6 7 E4
Poplar La RIPW IP8 20 B5
Poppy Cl CHTY IP2 21 F3
Portal Av KESG IP5 16 A4
Porter Rd IPSE IP3 33 F2
Portland Crs WDBR IP12 9 E4
Portman Rd IP IP1 2 C3
Port of Felixstowe Rd FX IP11 44 C2
Post Mill Cl FRAM/WMKT IP13 27 A4
IPNE IP4 3 K2
Post Mill Crs FRAM/WMKT * IP13 27 A4
Post Mill Gdns
FRAM/WMKT IP13 27 A4
Post Mill Orch
FRAM/WMKT IP13 27 A4
Post Office La WDBR IP12 16 C2
Pouch Ml FX IP11 43 B4
Pound La HADL IP7 36 C3
RIPS/CAP IP9 40 D4
RIPW IP8 29 E4
Powling Rd IPSE IP3 32 A1
Prentices La FRAM/WMKT IP13 8 D2
Preston Dr IP IP1 11 F3
Prestwick Av FX IP11 46 A3
Pretyman Rd FX IP11 47 D1
IPSE IP3 23 F5
Priestly Rd NHMKT IP6 4 B4
Primrose Hl CHTY IP2 21 F4
Primrose Wy NHMKT IP6 4 C5
Princedale Cl IP IP1 11 G4
Prince of Wales Dr CHTY IP2 30 C1

Princes Gdns *FX* IP11 45 F3
Princes Rd *FX* IP11 45 G4
Princes St *CHTY* IP2 2 B6
Princethorpe Rd *IPSE* IP3 23 G4
Priory Rd *FX* IP11 46 B4
Prittlewell Cl *CHTY* IP2 30 B2
The Promenade *FX* * IP11 45 F2
Prospect Pl *WDBR* * IP12 9 H2
Prospect Rd *IP* IP1 2 A1
Prospect St *IP* IP1 21 G2
Providence La *IP* IP1 21 G1
Providence St *IP* IP1 2 D3
Pump St *NHMKT* IP6 4 D4
Punchard Wy *FX* IP11 43 C4
Purdis Av *IPSE* IP3 33 F2
Purdis Farm La *IPSE* IP3 33 F1
Purdis Rd *KIR/NAC* IP10 34 B1
Purplett St *CHTY* IP2 3 F7
Pykenham Wy *HADL* IP7 36 D3
Pytches Cl *WDBR* IP12 9 G2
Pytches Rd *WDBR* IP12 9 G2

Q

Quadling St *IP* IP1 2 C5
Quantock Cl *KESG* IP5 24 B1
Quay Side *WDBR* IP12 9 H4
Quay St *WDBR* IP12 9 G4
Quebec Dr *KESG* IP5 14 D5
The Queech *RIPS/CAP* IP9 41 F1
Queens Av *WDBR* IP12 9 E4
Queensberry Rd *IPSE* IP3 32 A2
Queenscliffe Rd *CHTY* IP2 21 G5
Queensdale Cl *IP* IP1 11 H4
Queensgate Dr *IPNE* IP4 12 D5
Queen's Head La *WDBR* IP12 9 F3
Queen's Rd *FX* IP11 45 G3
Queens Rw *HADL* * IP7 36 D4
Queen's Sq *IPSE* IP3 32 B1
Queen St *FX* IP11 45 E1
HADL IP7 36 D3
IP IP1 2 D4
Queen's Wy *IPSE* IP3 32 B1
Quentin Cl *IP* IP1 11 E5
Quilter Dr *RIPW* IP8 29 G2
Quilter Rd *FX* IP11 45 H3
Quinton Rd *NHMKT* IP6 4 B4
Quintons Ct *NHMKT* * IP6 4 D4
Quinton's La *FX* IP11 46 A4
Quoits Fld *NHMKT* IP6 7 E4

R

Radcliffe Dr *CHTY* IP2 29 H1
Raeburn Rd *IPSE* IP3 31 H2
Raeburn Rd South *IPSE* IP3 31 G2
Railway Ap *FX* IP11 45 G2
Ramsey Cl *CHTY* IP2 30 C2
Ramsey Rd *HADL* IP7 37 F2
Ramsgate Dr *IPSE* IP3 23 F5
Randall Cl *KESG* IP5 25 G1
Rands Wy *IPSE* IP3 32 B2
Randwell Cl *IPNE* IP4 23 F3
Ranelagh Rd *CHTY* IP2 21 G3
FX IP11 45 G4
Ransome Cl *RIPW* IP8 20 A2
Ransome Crs *IPSE* IP3 32 B1
Ransome Rd *IPSE* IP3 32 B1
Ransomes Wy *IPSE* IP3 32 D3
Ransom Rd *WDBR* IP12 9 E2
Ranson Rd *NHMKT* IP6 4 B3
Ravensfield Rd *IP* IP1 11 E3
Ravens La *RIPW* IP8 10 A3
Ravens Wy *WDBR* IP12 16 B3
Ravenswood Av *IPSE* IP3 32 C3
Raven Wy *HADL* IP7 36 D5
Rayleigh Rd *IP* IP1 11 E4
Rayment Drift *KESG* IP5 25 E1
Reading Rd *IPNE* IP4 23 F1
Recreation Cl *FX* IP11 45 F1
Recreation La *FX* IP11 45 F1
Recreation Wy *IPSE* IP3 32 B1
Rectory La *KIR/NAC* IP10 42 B3
RIPW IP8 18 B5
Rectory Rd *CHTY* IP2 22 A5
Redan St *IP* IP1 2 B1
Red Barn Piece
FRAM/WMKT IP13 27 A4
Rede La *NHMKT* IP6 7 H3
Red Hill Rd *HADL* IP7 37 E1
Red House Cl *FX* IP11 43 A2
Red House Wk *KIR/NAC* IP10 39 G2
Red La *RIPS/CAP* IP9 41 E3
Red Sleeve *RIPS/CAP* IP9 40 D2
Redwing Cl *CHTY* IP2 20 D5
Redwold Cl *WDBR* IP12 16 C2
Reedland Wy *FX* IP11 44 D2
Reeve Gdns *KESG* IP5 25 E1
Reeve Ldg *FX* * IP11 43 B3
Regent St *IPNE* IP4 3 H3
Regina Cl *IPNE* IP4 23 F3
Reigate Cl *IPSE* IP3 23 F5
Rembrow Rd *RIPS/CAP* IP9 41 E2
Rendlesham Rd *FX* IP11 44 D2
IP IP1 2 A2
Renfrew Rd *IPNE* IP4 13 F4
Reynolds Av *IPSE* IP3 32 A3
Reynolds Ct *FX* IP11 44 D2
Reynolds Rd *IPSE* IP3 32 A3
Riby Rd *FX* IP11 45 F4
Richmond Rd *IP* IP1 21 F1
Riley Cl *IP* IP1 10 C4
Ringham Rd *IPNE* IP4 23 E2
Risby Cl *IPNE* IP4 23 F2
Ritabrook Rd *CHTY* IP2 30 A2
Riverside *FRAM/WMKT* IP13 8 A1
Riverside Rd *IP* IP1 21 F1
Rivers St *IPNE* IP4 3 K1
Robeck Rd *IPSE* IP3 31 G2
Robin Dr *CHTY* IP2 20 D5
Rodney Ct *WDBR* IP12 9 F1
Rogers Cl *FX* IP11 45 F1
Roma Av *KESG* IP5 16 C5
Roman Wy *FX* IP11 46 B3
Romney Rd *IPSE* IP3 32 A3
Ropes Dr *KESG* IP5 14 D5
Rope Wk *IPNE* IP4 3 G4
Rosebery Rd *FX* IP11 45 H3
IPNE IP4 3 K4
Rosecroft Rd *IP* IP1 11 G3
Rose Hl *FRAM/WMKT* IP13 27 A3
Rosehill Crs *IPSE* IP3 3 K6
Rose La *IPNE* IP4 2 E5
Rosemary Av *FX* IP11 45 H1
Rose Wk *NHMKT* IP6 4 C5
Ross Rd *IPNE* IP4 13 F4
Roundridge Rd *RIPS/CAP* IP9 41 F1
Roundwood Rd *IPNE* IP4 23 E1
Rousies Cl *HADL* IP7 37 E3
Routh Av *IPSE* IP3 33 F2
Rowanhayes Cl *CHTY* IP2 21 H5
Rowarth Av *KESG* IP5 25 E1
Roxburgh Rd *IPNE* IP4 13 F4
Roy Av *IPNE* IP4 23 F3
Roy Cl *KESG* IP5 24 D1
Royston Dr *CHTY* IP2 29 H1
Rubens Rd *IPSE* IP3 32 A2
Rudlands *RIPW* IP8 29 G2
Rue's La *FX* IP11 46 A1
Runnacles Wy *FX* IP11 44 D2
Rushbury Cl *IPNE* IP4 13 F5
Rushmeadow Wy *FX* IP11 46 B2
Rushmere Rd *IPNE* IP4 23 E1
Rushmere St *KESG* IP5 13 H4
Ruskin Rd *IPNE* IP4 22 D3
Russell Rd *FX* IP11 45 F5
IP IP1 2 B5
Rydal Av *FX* IP11 46 B2
Rydal Wk *IPSE* IP3 32 C1
Rye Cl *IPSE* IP3 23 H4
Rylands *RIPS/CAP* IP9 41 E1

S

Saddlers Meadow
FRAM/WMKT IP13 27 B2
Saddlers Pl *KESG* IP5 26 A1
St Agnes Wy *KESG* IP5 24 B1
St Andrews Cl *IPNE* IP4 23 H3
St Andrew's Rd *FX* IP11 45 G2
St Annes Cl *FRAM/WMKT* IP13 8 D5
St Aubyns Rd *IPNE* IP4 23 E3
St Augustine Rd *IPSE* IP3 23 H4
St Augustine's Gdn *IPSE* IP3 23 G5
St Austell Cl *KESG* IP5 24 C2
St Catherine's Ct *CHTY* IP2 30 A2
St Clements Church La
IPNE * IP4 3 G5
St David's Rd *IPSE* IP3 23 F5
St Edmunds Cl *WDBR* IP12 9 E4
St Edmund's Pl *IP* IP1 12 A5
St Edmund's Rd *FX* IP11 45 E5
IP IP1 11 H5
St Francis Ct *IP* * IP1 2 D4
St George's Rd *FX* IP11 46 A3
St George's St *IP* IP1 2 D2
St Georges Ter *FX* * IP11 46 A3
St Gotthards Av *KESG* IP5 16 C5
St Helen's St *IPNE* IP4 3 H3
St Isidores *KESG* IP5 25 F1
St Ives Cl *KESG* IP5 24 C2
St Johns Ct *FX* IP11 45 F3
St John's Hl *WDBR* IP12 9 G3
St John's Rd *IPNE* IP4 22 D2
St John's St *WDBR* IP12 9 G3
St John's Ter *WDBR* IP12 9 G3
St Lawrence Wy *KESG* IP5 14 D5
St Leonards Rd *IPSE* IP3 23 F5
St Margarets Pln *IP* IP1 2 E2
St Margaret's St *IPNE* IP4 3 F2
St Martins Ct *KESG* IP5 25 G1
St Martins Gn *FX* IP11 43 A2
St Mary's Cl *FX* IP11 43 B5
RIPW IP8 10 A4
St Mary's Crs *FX* IP11 45 E1
St Mary's Gdns *NHMKT* IP6 4 D2
St Marys Pk *KIR/NAC* IP10 35 E3
St Mary's Rd *NHMKT* IP6 4 D2
St Marys Wy *NHMKT* IP6 12 D1
St Matthew's St *IP* IP1 2 C2
St Michael's Cl *KESG* IP5 24 C2
St Nicholas St *IP* IP1 2 D4
St Olaves Rd *KESG* IP5 15 E5
St Osyth Cl *CHTY* IP2 30 B3
St Peter's Av *NHMKT* IP6 7 E3
St Peter's Cl *FRAM/WMKT* IP13 8 D4
NHMKT IP6 6 D3
St Peter's Ct *NHMKT* IP6 6 D3
St Peter's St *IPNE* IP4 2 E4
Salehurst Rd *IPSE* IP3 24 A5
Salisbury Rd *IPSE* IP3 23 E5
Sallows Cl *IP* IP1 21 F1
Sally Wood's La *NHMKT* IP6 5 F3
Salters Gdns *FRAM/WMKT* IP13 27 A3
Salthouse La *IPNE* IP4 3 F5
Samford Pl *RIPW* IP8 20 B2
Samuel Ct *IPNE* IP4 3 G3
Sandhurst Av *IPSE* IP3 22 D4
Sandling Crs *IPNE* IP4 24 A3
Sandown Rd *IP* IP1 11 G2
Sandpiper Rd *CHTY* IP2 30 A1
Sandpit Cl *IPNE* IP4 24 B3
Sandringham Cl *CHTY* IP2 30 B1
Sandy Cl *FX* IP11 43 B2
Sandyhill La *IPSE* IP3 31 G2
Sandy La *FRAM/WMKT* IP13 15 F1
WDBR IP12 16 D1
Sapling Pl *IPNE* IP4 24 A3
Sawmill La *KIR/NAC* IP10 33 H5
Sawston Cl *CHTY* IP2 30 C1
Sawyers Cl *RIPS/CAP* IP9 41 E2
Saxon Cl *FX* IP11 46 B3
Saxon La *RIPW* IP8 28 B3
Saxon Pk *NHMKT* * IP6 4 A4
Saxon Wy *WDBR* IP12 9 G2
Schneider Cl *FX* IP11 47 B2
School Cl *HADL* IP7 37 E4
RIPS/CAP IP9 41 E2
School Hl *RIPW* IP8 28 D3
School La *WDBR* IP12 16 C2
School St *NHMKT* IP6 4 C4
Schreiber Rd *IPNE* IP4 23 F1
Scopes Rd *KESG* IP5 15 E5
Scott Rd *IPSE* IP3 32 B2
Scrivener Dr *RIPW* IP8 29 G1
Sea Rd *FX* IP11 45 F5
Seaton Rd *FX* IP11 45 E2
Seckford Cl *IPNE* IP4 24 B3
Seckford Hall Rd *WDBR* IP12 8 D5
Seckford St *WDBR* IP12 9 F3
Second Av *FX* IP11 43 B5
Selkirk Rd *IPNE* IP4 13 G5
Selvale Wy *FX* IP11 45 E3
Selwyn Cl *CHTY* IP2 2 D7
Serpentine Rd *IPSE* IP3 32 B1
Seven Cottages La *KESG* IP5 13 G4
Seven Gardens Rd
FRAM/WMKT IP13 27 C2
Seven Hills *KIR/NAC* * IP10 34 B4
Severn Rd *IPSE* IP3 22 D5
Sewell Wontner Cl *KESG* IP5 14 D5
Seymour Rd *CHTY* IP2 2 D7
Shackleton Rd *IPSE* IP3 23 F5
Shaftesbury Sq *IPNE* * IP4 3 G4
Shafto Rd *IP* IP1 11 E5
Shakespeare Rd *IP* IP1 11 E2
Shamrock Av *CHTY* IP2 21 E4
Shannon Rd *IPSE* IP3 32 A3
Shaw Valley Rd *WDBR* IP12 16 B3
Shearman Rd *HADL* IP7 37 F4
Shelbourne Cl *KESG* IP5 25 F1
Sheldrake Dr *CHTY* IP2 30 A1
Shelley St *CHTY* IP2 2 E7
Shenley Rd *IPSE* IP3 32 B2
Shenstone Dr *IP* IP1 11 G2
Shepherd Dr *RIPW* IP8 29 G1
Sheppards Wy *KESG* IP5 25 F1
Sherborne Av *IPNE* IP4 13 E3
Sherrington Rd *IP* IP1 11 G5
Sherwood Flds *KESG* IP5 25 E1
Shetland Cl *IPNE* IP4 13 E5
Ship La *RIPW* IP8 10 B4
Ship Launch Rd *IPSE* IP3 22 B5
Shire Hall Tard *IPNE* IP4 3 F5
Shirley Cl *IP* IP1 11
Shore La *KIR/NAC* IP10 38
Shortlands *CHTY* IP2 29
Shotley Cl *FX* IP11 44
RIPW IP8 29
Shrubbery Cl *FX* IP11 45
Shrubbery Rd
FRAM/WMKT IP13 8
Shrubland Av *IP* IP1 11
Shrubland Dr *IPNE* IP4 24
Sidegate Av *IPNE* IP4 13
Sidegate La *IPNE* IP4 13
Sidegate La West *IPNE* IP4 12
Silent St *IPNE* IP4 2
Silk Mill Cl *HADL* IP7 36
Silverdale Cl *IP* IP1 11
Silver Hl *RIPW* IP8 18
Simons Rd *WDBR* IP12 9
Sinclair Dr *CHTY* IP2 22
Sir Alf Ramsey Wy *IP* IP1 2
Sirdar Rd *IP* IP1 21
Skipper Cl *RIPW* IP8 30
Skipper Rd *CHTY* IP2 30
Skylark La *RIPW* IP8 29
The Slade *NHMKT* IP6 7
Slade St *IPNE* IP4 3
Sleaford Cl *CHTY* IP2 21
Smart St *IPNE* IP4 3
Smithers Cl *RIPS/CAP* IP9 41
Smithfield *WDBR* IP12 9
Smiths Pl *KESG* IP5 25
Snowcroft *RIPS/CAP* IP9 41
Snowdon Rd *CHTY* IP2 30
Soane St *IPNE* IP4 3
Somerset Rd *IPNE* IP4 12
Sorrel Cl *CHTY* IP2 21
South Cl *IPNE* IP4 12
South Hl *FX* IP11 45
South St *IP* IP1 2
Speedwell Rd *CHTY* IP2 21
Spenser Rd *IP* IP1 11
Spinner Cl *IP* IP1 10
The Spinney *IPNE* IP4 24
Spitfire Cl *IPSE* IP3 32
Spooners Cl *HADL* IP7 36
Springfield Av *FX* IP11 45
Springfield La *IP* IP1 11
Springhurst Cl *IPNE* IP4 22
Springland Cl *IPNE* IP4 23
Spring Meadow *NHMKT* IP6 14
Spring Rd *IPNE* IP4 3
RIPW IP8 28
Sprites End *FX* IP11 43
Spriteshall La *FX* IP11 43
Sprites La *RIPW* IP8 29
Sproughton Rd *RIPW* IP8 20
Squires La *KESG* IP5 16
The Squirrels *RIPS/CAP* IP9 41
Stable Ct *KESG* IP5 16
Stamford Cl *CHTY* IP2 30
Stammers Pl *KESG* IP5 25
Stanley Av *IPSE* IP3 23
Stanley Rd *FX* IP11 45
Starfield Cl *IPNE* IP4 23
Star La *IPNE* IP4 2
Station Rd *FX* IP11 43
HADL IP7 37
NHMKT IP6 6
RIPS/CAP IP9 41
WDBR IP12 9
Station St *CHTY* IP2 22
Station Yd *NHMKT* IP6 4
Steggall Cl *NHMKT* IP6 4
Stella Maris *CHTY* IP2 20
Stennetts Cl *FX* IP11 43
Stephen Rd *KESG* IP5 15
Stephen's Ct *IPNE* IP4 23
Stevenson Rd *IP* IP1 2
Stewart Young Gv *KESG* IP5 25
Stockmers End *RIPS/CAP* IP9 41
Stockton Cl *HADL* IP7 37
Stoke Br *IP* IP1 2
Stokebridge Maltings *IPSE* * IP3 2
Stoke Hall Rd *CHTY* IP2 2
Stoke Park Dr *CHTY* IP2 30
Stoke Quay *IPSE* IP3 3
Stoke St *CHTY* IP2 2
Stollery Cl *KESG* IP5 25
Stonechat Rd *CHTY* IP2 20
Stonecroft Gdns *CHTY* * IP2 21
Stonegrove Rd *FX* IP11 47
Stonehouse Rd *HADL* IP7 36
Stone Lodge La *CHTY* IP2 21
Stone Lodge La West *CHTY* IP2 21
Stone Lodge Wk *CHTY* IP2 21
Stone St *HADL* IP7 36
Stopford Ct *IP* IP1 2
Stour Av *FX* IP11 45
Stowmarket Rd *NHMKT* IP6 6
Stradbroke Rd *IPNE* IP4 23

aight Rd KIR/NAC IP10 34 A3
Strand CHTY IP2 31 E3
atford Rd IP IP1 11 F3
attonhall Drift
IR/NAC IP10 39 H4
Street FRAM/WMKT IP13 15 F1
RAM/WMKT IP13 27 A3
IR/NAC IP10 39 E1
IPS/CAP IP9 30 C5
IPS/CAP IP9 40 D2
IPW IP8 10 A3
IPW IP8 28 D3
IPW IP8 29 G5
VDBR IP12 16 C2
art Cl FX IP11 46 B2
PNE IP4 3 K1
bbs Cl IPSE IP3 32 A2
rdee Av IPSE IP3 23 F5
-Station Rd FX IP11 44 D5
dbourne Rd FX IP11 44 D2
dbury Rd FX IP11 44 C3
ffolk Coast & Heaths Pth
X IP11 45 H4
PSE IP3 32 A5
IR/NAC IP10 39 E3
IPS/CAP IP9 38 A5
ffolk Rd IPNE IP4 3 G1
mmerfield Cl IPNE IP4 13 H5
nderland Rd FX IP11 47 B2
nfield Cl IPNE IP4 23 F2
n La WDBR IP12 9 G3
nningdale Av IPNE IP4 23 H3
nningdale Dr FX IP11 45 H1
nray Av FX IP11 45 H1
rbiton Rd IP IP1 21 F1
rrey Rd FX IP11 45 F3
P IP1 21 G2
tton Cl WDBR IP12 9 H3
allow Cl FX IP11 46 A2
allow Rd CHTY IP2 20 C5
allowtail Cl RIPW IP8 30 A3
an Cl KESG IP5 26 A1
an Hl RIPW IP8 29 E1
an La NHMKT IP6 12 C1
ansea Av CHTY IP2 30 D2
atchway Cl IPSE IP3 32 B3
inburne Rd IP IP1 11 E2
inton Cl CHTY IP2 29 H2
camore Cl RIPW IP8 29 G2

T

cket St IPNE IP4 2 E4
con Rd FX IP11 47 C1
llboys Cl KESG IP5 15 E5
nners Vw IP IP1 21 F1
nyard Ct WDBR IP12 9 G4
rn Hows Cl FX IP11 46 B3
smania Rd IPNE IP4 23 H2
unton Cl IP IP1 11 H1
unton Rd FX IP11 45 F2
vern St IP IP1 2 E3
wney Cl RIPS/CAP IP9 41 E2
yler Cl HADL IP7 36 D4
yler Rd HADL IP7 36 D4
al Cl CHTY IP2 20 D5
mple Rd IPSE IP3 23 G4
nby Rd CHTY IP2 30 D2
nnyson Cl WDBR IP12 9 E2
nnyson Rd IPNE IP4 22 D3
nth Rd KIR/NAC IP10 35 F5
rn Rd CHTY IP2 30 A1
e Terrace HADL * IP7 37 E2
ackeray Rd IP IP1 11 E2
anet Rd IPNE IP4 23 F2
eatre St WDBR IP12 9 F3
eberton Rd IPSE IP3 32 B2
eobald Cl NHMKT IP6 4 C3
etford Rd IP IP1 21 F1
istle Cl CHTY IP2 21 F4
omas Av FX IP11 43 C4
omas Walls Cl
FRAM/WMKT IP13 27 B3
ompson Rd IP IP1 11 F5
orney Rd RIPS/CAP IP9 41 E1
ornhayes Cl CHTY IP2 21 G5
ornhill Rd NHMKT IP6 7 E2
ornley Dr IPNE IP4 13 G5
ornley Rd FX IP11 46 A5
orn Wy FX IP11 45 E3
e Thoroughfare WDBR IP12 9 G4
oroughfare IP * IP1 2 D3
orpe's Hl RIPW IP8 19 E5
readneedle St HADL IP7 36 D3
rough Duncans WDBR IP12 9 E5
rough Jollys KESG IP5 15 F5
hurmans La FX IP11 43 B4
hurston Ct FX IP11 44 C3
Tide Mill Wy WDBR IP12 9 H4
Timperley Cl HADL IP7 36 D2
Timperley Rd HADL IP7 37 E2
Timperleys RIPW IP8 18 B5
Tinabrook Cl CHTY IP2 30 A2
Tinker's La HADL IP7 36 D5
Tintern Cl CHTY IP2 30 C1
Tokio Rd IPNE IP4 23 E2
Toller Rd IPSE IP3 22 C5
Toll Gate Rd RIPS/CAP IP9 41 E2
Tolworth Rd IPNE IP4 23 E2
Tomline Rd FX IP11 45 G3
IPSE IP3 23 E3
Toppesfield Cl HADL IP7 36 D4
Top St WDBR IP12 16 C1
Tortoiseshell Cl CHTY IP2 30 A3
Tovell's Rd IPNE IP4 22 D2
Tower Mill La HADL IP7 37 E3
Tower Mill Rd IP IP1 21 F1
Tower Ramparts IP IP1 2 E2
Tower Rd FX IP11 45 F4
Tower St IP IP1 2 E3
Trafalgar Cl IPNE IP4 22 D2
Tranmere Gv IP IP1 11 F3
Trefoil Cl CHTY IP2 21 F4
Trent Rd IPSE IP3 31 H1
Trimley Rd KIR/NAC IP10 42 B4
Trinity Av FX IP11 44 B4
Trinity Cl KESG IP5 24 B1
WDBR IP12 8 D5
Trinity St IPSE IP3 3 J7
Trinity Terminal FX * IP11 44 B5
Troon Gdns IPNE IP4 13 F5
Truro Crs KESG IP5 24 C2
Tuddenham Av IPNE IP4 3 H1
Tuddenham La KESG IP5 13 F3
Tuddenham Rd IPNE IP4 3 G1
Turin St CHTY IP2 2 E7
Turino Av KESG IP5 16 C5
Turner Gdns WDBR IP12 8 D5
Turner Gv KESG IP5 15 F5
Turner Rd IPSE IP3 32 A3
Turnpike Rd WDBR IP12 9 H2
Turret La IPNE IP4 2 E5
Twelve Acre Ap KESG IP5 24 D1
Two Acres RIPS/CAP IP9 41 F1
Tylers Gn FX IP11 43 C5
Tyler St CHTY IP2 3 F7
Tyrone Cl IP IP1 10 D3

U

Ullswater Av FX IP11 46 B2
Ulster Av IP IP1 10 D4
Undercliff Rd East FX IP11 46 A5
Undercliff Rd West FX IP11 45 G4
Union St IPNE * IP4 3 F3
Unity St IPSE IP3 3 J7
Upland Rd IPNE IP4 23 E2
Upper Barclay St IPNE IP4 3 F4
Upper Brook St IPNE IP4 2 E4
Upperfield Dr FX IP11 45 H1
Upper High St IP IP1 2 D1
Upper Moorfield Rd
WDBR IP12 9 E2
Upper Orwell St IPNE IP4 3 F4
Upsons Wy KESG IP5 15 G5
Upton Cl IPNE IP4 3 J3
Uvedale Gdns NHMKT IP6 4 D4
Uxbridge Crs IPSE IP3 32 C2

V

Valiant Rd KESG IP5 26 A1
Valley Cl IP IP1 12 A4
Valley Farm La HADL IP7 37 H4
Valley Rd IP IP1 11 H5
Valleyview Dr IPNE IP4 24 B4
Valley Wk FX IP11 45 F3
Vandyck Rd IPSE IP3 32 A3
Vaughan St CHTY IP2 2 E7
Ventris Cl CHTY IP2 20 D3
Vere Gdns IP IP1 12 A3
Vermont Crs IPNE IP4 3 G1
Vermont Rd IPNE IP4 22 B1
Vernon St CHTY IP2 2 E7
Vicarage Cl RIPW IP8 10 B4
Vicarage Hl WDBR IP12 9 G3
Vicarage La RIPW IP8 10 B4
Vicarage Rd FX IP11 44 D3
Victoria Rd FX IP11 45 F4
WDBR IP12 9 G3
Victoria St FX IP11 45 G3
IP IP1 2 A2
Victory Rd IPNE IP4 23 E1
View Point Rd FX IP11 47 B3
Viking Cl WDBR IP12 16 C3
Viking Hts WDBR IP12 16 C3
Vincent Cl IP IP1 11 E5
Violet Cl CHTY IP2 21 F4

W

Wades Gv KESG IP5 25 G1
Wadgate Rd FX IP11 45 E3
Wadhurst Rd IPSE IP3 23 H5
Waggoners Ct WDBR * IP12 9 F3
Wainwright Gdns NHMKT IP6 6 B2
Wainwright Wy KESG IP5 15 F5
Waldringfield Rd WDBR IP12 16 D3
The Walk FX IP11 45 E2
IP IP1 2 E3
KESG IP5 14 D5
Walker Cl IPNE IP4 23 G3
Wallace Rd IP IP1 11 E5
Waller's Gv CHTY IP2 21 F4
Walnut Cl FX IP11 46 B2
Waltham Cl CHTY IP2 30 C1
Walton Av FX IP11 44 C4
Wardley Cl CHTY IP2 29 H2
Ward Rd RIPW IP8 29 F1
Wareham Av IPSE IP3 23 H5
Warren Cha KESG IP5 25 G1
Warren Heath Av IPSE IP3 32 D1
Warren Heath Rd IPSE IP3 32 D1
Warren Hill Rd WDBR IP12 9 E4
Warren La KESG IP5 26 A1
Warrington Rd IP IP1 21 H1
Warwick Av WDBR IP12 9 F2
Warwick Rd IPNE IP4 3 J2
Waterford Rd IP IP1 10 D3
Waterloo Rd IP IP1 21 G1
Waterworks St IPNE IP4 3 G4
Waveney Rd FX IP11 45 E4
IP IP1 11 E5
Weaver Cl IP IP1 10 D5
Weavers Cl HADL IP7 36 D3
Weavers Wy NHMKT IP6 6 D3
Webbs Ct KESG IP5 25 E1
Weir Pl KIR/NAC IP10 42 B2
Welbeck Cl FX IP11 43 C5
Wellesley Rd IPNE IP4 22 D3
Wellington St IP IP1 2 A1
Wells Cl IPNE IP4 3 H3
Wenham La RCOLE CO7 40 A3
Wenham Rd RIPW IP8 28 B4
Wentworth Cl HADL IP7 37 F4
Wentworth Dr FX IP11 46 A3
RIPW IP8 29 G1
Wesel Av FX IP11 44 D4
Wesley Wy IP IP1 21 F1
Westbourne Rd IP IP1 11 F4
Westbury Rd IPNE IP4 13 F5
West End Rd IP IP1 2 B5
Westerfield Ct IPNE * IP4 22 B1
Westerfield Rd IPNE IP4 3 F1
Western Av FX IP11 46 B3
Western Cl IPNE IP4 24 B4
Westgate St IP IP1 2 D3
Westholme Cl WDBR IP12 9 F4
Westholme Rd IP IP1 11 G4
Westland KESG IP5 26 A1
West Lawn IPNE IP4 13 F5
Westleton Wy FX IP11 44 D2
West Mdw IP IP1 10 C1
West Mill Gn RIPS/CAP IP9 41 H5
Westminster Cl IPNE IP4 23 F3
Westmorland Rd FX IP11 46 B2
West Rd IPSE IP3 33 E3
Westwood Av IP IP1 11 G5
Wetherby Cl IP IP1 11 H2
Wexford Rd IP IP1 10 D3
Weymouth Rd IPNE IP4 22 D2
Wharfedale Rd IP IP1 11 G4
The Wheelwrights FX IP11 43 C4
Wherry La IPSE * IP3 3 F5
Wherstead Rd CHTY IP2 22 A5
Whights' Cnr RIPW IP8 29 E2
Whinchat Cl CHTY IP2 20 D5
Whinfield KESG IP5 26 A1
Whinfield Ct KESG IP5 16 A5
The Whinneys KESG IP5 15 F5
Whinyard Wy FX IP11 46 B2
Whitby Rd IPNE IP4 12 D5
White Elm St IPSE IP3 3 J6
White Foot La
FRAM/WMKT IP13 27 B1
White Horse Cl FX IP11 46 A3
White Horse Rd RIPS/CAP IP9 41 F2
Whitehouse Cottages FX * IP11 46 A2
White House Rd IP IP1 10 C2
Whitethorn Rd IPSE IP3 33 F2
Whitland Cl CHTY IP2 30 C3
Whittle Rd CHTY IP2 21 F2
Whitton Church La IP IP1 11 E1
Whitton Leyer RIPW IP8 10 C3
Whitworth Cl CHTY IP2 29 H1
Wickhambrook Ct FX IP11 44 C3
Wicklow Rd IP IP1 10 D3
Widgeon Cl CHTY IP2 21 F5
Wigmore Cl CHTY IP2 30 B2
Wilberforce St IP IP1 2 A2
Wilderness Hl RIPW IP8 18 A5
Wilderness La WDBR IP12 9 G2
Wilding Dr KESG IP5 25 F1
Wilding Rd RIPW IP8 29 G2
Wilkinson Dr KESG IP5 25 E2
Wilkinson Wy WDBR IP12 9 G2
William Booth Wy FX IP11 44 D2
Williamsport Wy NHMKT IP6 5 E5
William St IP IP1 2 E2
Willoughby Rd CHTY IP2 2 C6
Willow Cl NHMKT IP6 7 E4
Willowcroft Rd IP IP1 11 G3
Wilmslow Av WDBR IP12 9 E3
Wilmslow Dr RIPW IP8 29 G1
Wilson Rd HADL IP7 37 E4
RIPW IP8 29 F2
Wimborne Av IPSE IP3 23 H4
Wimpole Cl KESG IP5 24 B2
Wincanton Cl IPNE IP4 13 E4
Winchester Gdns NHMKT IP6 7 F2
Winchester Wy CHTY IP2 30 B3
Windermere Cl IPSE IP3 32 B3
Windermere Rd FX IP11 46 B2
Winding Piece RIPS/CAP IP9 41 E2
Windmill Hl RIPS/CAP IP9 40 C2
Windrush Rd KESG IP5 15 E5
Windsor Rd FX IP11 45 E4
IP IP1 21 F1
Winfrith Rd IPSE IP3 23 H4
Wingfield St IPNE IP4 3 F4
Winston Av IPNE IP4 13 G5
Winston Cl FX IP11 44 D2
Withipoll St IP IP1 3 F2
Wolsey Gdns FX IP11 45 G4
Wolsey St IP IP1 2 D5
Wolton Rd KESG IP5 25 E1
Wolves Farm La HADL IP7 37 G1
Woodbridge Rd
FRAM/WMKT IP13 27 A2
IPNE IP4 3 H3
IPNE IP4 23 H1
KESG IP5 14 B5
WDBR IP12 16 E4
Woodbridge Rd East IPNE IP4 23 G1
Woodcock Rd CHTY IP2 30 A1
Woodhouse La KIR/NAC IP10 34 A1
Woodhouse Sq IPNE * IP4 3 G4
Woodlands HADL IP7 36 B2
Woodlands Wy RIPW IP8 10 B1
Woodpecker Rd CHTY IP2 20 D5
Woodrush Rd IPSE IP3 32 D1
Woods La WDBR IP12 9 H1
Woodspring Cl CHTY IP2 30 C1
Woodstone Av IP IP1 12 A4
Woodthorpe Cl HADL IP7 37 F4
Woodthorpe Rd HADL IP7 37 E4
Woodville Rd IPNE IP4 3 K4
Woollards Cl IP IP1 21 G2
Woolner Cl NHMKT IP6 6 D3
Woolnough Rd WDBR IP12 9 F2
The Woolnoughs KESG IP5 25 F1
Woolverstone Cl CHTY IP2 29 H2
Worcester Rd IPSE IP3 32 A3
Wordsworth Crs IP IP1 11 E2
Workshop La KIR/NAC IP10 38 D1
Worsley Cl CHTY IP2 29 H1
Wren Av CHTY IP2 20 D5
Wrens Pk FX IP11 46 B2
Wright La KESG IP5 15 F5
Wright Rd IPSE IP3 32 C1
Wroxham Rd IPSE IP3 22 D5
Wye Rd IPSE IP3 23 E5
Wykes Bishop St IPSE IP3 3 H7
Wynterton Cl IPSE IP3 32 B2
Wyvern Rd IPSE IP3 32 C2

Y

Yarmouth Rd IP IP1 21 F2
Yeoman Crs HADL IP7 37 E4
Yeoman Rd FX IP11 44 D4
Yeoman Wy HADL IP7 37 E4
Yew Ct CHTY IP2 21 G5
Yewtree Gv KESG IP5 24 B1
Yewtree Ri RIPW IP8 29 G2
York Crs NHMKT IP6 7 E3
York Rd FX IP11 45 G3
IPSE IP3 23 E4
KESG IP5 26 B2

The Abbey School *WDBR* IP12 9 G3
Alpha Business Park *IP* IP1 11 E2
Amberfield School *KIR/NAC* IP10 34 A5
Ancient House *IP* IP1 2 E3
Bartlet Hospital *FX* IP11 45 H3
BBC Radio Suffolk *IP* IP1 2 C2
Beacon Hill Primary School *WDBR* IP12 16 A3
Beacon Hill Special School *CHTY* IP2 21 F5
Bealings School *FRAM/WMKT* IP13 15 F1
Belstead School *RIPW* IP8 29 G1
Birchwood County Primary School *KESG* IP5 26 A1
Blackfriars Priory Hall *IPNE* IP4 3 F4
Bosmere Primary School *NHMKT* IP6 4 B4
The Brackenbury Sports Centre *FX* IP11 46 A4
Bramford CE Primary School *RIPW* IP8 10 A4
Brewery Museum *IPSE* IP3 22 C5
Bridge Trading Estate *NHMKT* IP6 6 D3
Brittania Primary School *IPNE* IP4 23 F3
Broke Hall Primary School *IPNE* IP4 24 A3
Brook Craft Market *IP* IP1 2 E3
Brookhouse Business Park *CHTY* IP2 21 F2
Broom Hill Swimming Pool *IP* IP1 11 G5
Broomvale Business Centre *RIPW* IP8 6 C5
Bucklesham Primary School *KIR/NAC* IP10 35 F3
Buttermarket Shopping Centre *IP* IP1 2 E4
Capel St Mary CE Primary School *RIPS/CAP* IP9 41 E2
Cardinal Park *IP* IP1 2 D5
Castle Hill J & I School *IP* IP1 11 G2
Causton School *FX* IP11 45 E1
Chantry Clinic *CHTY* IP2 21 E5
Chantry High School *CHTY* IP2 21 F5
Chantry J & I School *CHTY* IP2 21 E4
Chirstchurch Mansion *IP* IP1 2 E2
Civil Service Sports Club *KIR/NAC* IP10 34 A2
Claydon Business Park *NHMKT* IP6 6 C2
Claydon High School *NHMKT* IP6 7 E4
Claydon Primary School *NHMKT* IP6 7 E3
Cliff Lane Primary School *IPSE* IP3 22 C5
College Annexe *IPNE* IP4 3 F5
Colneis Junior School *FX* IP11 45 H1
Copdock Cricket Club *RIPW* IP8 28 D4
Copdock Primary School *RIPW* IP8 28 D3
Copleston High School *IPNE* IP4 23 G3
Corn Exchange *HADL* IP7 36 D4
Corn Exchange & Film Theatre *IP* IP1 2 D3
Crown Pools *IP* IP1 2 D2
Dale Hall Primary School *IP* IP1 11 H3
Deben High School *FX* IP11 45 F3
Deben Swimming Pool *WDBR* IP12 9 G4
Downing Primary School *CHTY* IP2 30 B1
Eastgate Shopping Centre *IPNE* IP4 3 F3
Elton Park Business Centre *CHTY* IP2 21 E2
Elton Park Industrial Estate *CHTY* IP2 21 E2
Euro Retail Park *IPSE* IP3 32 D2
Fairfield Infant School *FX* IP11 45 G2
Farlingaye County High School *WDBR* IP12 9 E2
Farthing Road Industrial Estate *IP* IP1 20 D1
Felixstowe & Walton FC *FX* IP11 45 H1
Felixstowe Cemetery *FX* IP11 45 E3
Felixstowe Ferry Golf Club *FX* IP11 46 C2
Felixstowe General Hospital *FX* IP11 45 G3
Felixstowe International College *FX* IP11 46 A4
Felixstowe Leisure Centre *FX* IP11 45 F4
Felixstowe Pier *FX* IP11 45 G4
Felixstowe RFC *FX* IP11 45 E4
Fore Street Pool *IPNE* IP4 3 G5
Foxhall Heath Stadium *IPNE* IP4 24 C3
Fozel Theatre *HADL* IP7 36 C4
The Framlingham Swimming Club *WDBR* IP12 9 G4
Gainsborough Sports Centre *IPSE* IP3 32 B3
Gorseland Primary School *KESG* IP5 15 H5
Grange Primary School *FX* IP11 44 D3
Greenwich Business Park *IPSE* IP3 22 C5
Grundisburgh County Primary School *FRAM/WMKT* IP13 27 A3
The Guildhall *HADL* IP7 36 C4
Gusford Primary School *CHTY* IP2 29 H2
Hadleigh Business Park *HADL* IP7 37 H5
Hadleigh Health Centre *HADL* IP7 36 C4
Hadleigh High School *HADL* IP7 37 E4
Hadleigh Primary School *HADL* IP7 36 D4
Hadleigh Road Industrial Estate *CHTY* IP2 21 E2
Hadleigh RUFC *HADL* IP7 36 D5
Hadleigh Swimming Pool *HADL* IP7 36 D3
Halifax Primary School *CHTY* IP2 30 D1
Handford Hall Primary School *IP* IP1 21 G2
Heath Primary School *KESG* IP5 24 D1
Heathside Special School *IPNE* IP4 23 G2
Hillside Community Primary School *CHTY* IP2 22 A5
Hintlesham & Chattisham CEVCP School *RIPW* IP8 18 C5
HM Customs & Excise *IPNE* IP4 2 E4
Holywells High School *IPSE* IP3 32 B2
Ipswich Airport (disused) *IPSE* IP3 32 C4
Ipswich Crematorium *IPNE* IP4 12 D5
Ipswich Golf Club *IPSE* IP3 33 F1
Ipswich Hospital *IPNE* IP4 23 G2
Ipswich Museums & Art Gallery *IP* IP1 2 D2
Ipswich Preparatory School *IP* IP1 21 H1
Ipswich Regent Theatre *IPNE* IP4 3 G3
Ipswich RUFC *KESG* IP5 13 F3
Ipswich School *IP* IP1 11 H5
Ipswich Sports Club *IP* IP1 12 A4
Ipswich Town FC (Portman Road) *IP* IP1 2 B4
Ipswich Transport Museum *IPSE* IP3 32 C1
Kesgrave County High School *KESG* IP5 15 E4
Kings Fleet Primary School *FX* IP11 46 A3
Kyson Primary School *WDBR* IP12 8 D4
Lady Lane Industrial Estate *HADL* IP7 37 E2
Lancaster Ipswich Athletics Track & Stadium *IPNE* IP4 12 D3
Landguard Fort *FX* IP11 47 A4
Langer Park Industrial Estate *FX* IP11 45 E5
Langer Primary School *FX* IP11 45 E5
Lion Barn Industrial Estate *NHMKT* IP6 4 D4
Low House Touring Caravan Centre *KIR/NAC* IP10 34 A2
Maidenhall Sports Centre *CHTY* IP2 31 E1
Maidstone County Infant School *FX* IP11 45 E2
Mallard House Business Centre *FRAM/WMKT* IP13 15 F2
Melton Primary School *WDBR* IP12 9 H1
Moon & Sixpence *WDBR* IP12 17 E5
Morland Primary School *IPSE* IP3 32 A3
Murrayfield Primary School *IPSE* IP3 23 E5
Nacton CE VC Primary School *KIR/NAC* IP10 38 D1
Nature Reserve *FX* IP11 47 A5
Needham Market Middle School *NHMKT* IP6 4 C4
New Cemetery *IPNE* IP4 12 C5
New Industrial Site *RIPW* IP8 6 C4
Northgate County High School *IPNE* IP4 12 D4
Northgate Sports Centre *IPNE* IP4 12 D4
Odeon Cinema *IPNE* IP4 3 F3
Old Cemetery *IPNE* IP4 12 C5
Old Customs House *IPSE* IP3 3 F5
Orwell Business Centre *IPSE* IP3 31 G1
Orwell Country Park *IPSE* IP3 31 H3
Orwell High School *FX* IP11 45 E2
Orwell Junior School *IPSE* IP3 31 H2
Orwell Park School *KIR/NAC* IP10 38 D3
Orwell Retail Park *CHTY* IP2 21 F3
Orwell Yacht Club *CHTY* IP2 31 E2
Palace Cinema *FX* IP11 45 G3
Peewit Caravan Park *FX* IP11 45 E5
Portmans Walk Industrial Centre *IP* IP1 2 A4
Priory Park *KIR/NAC* IP10 32 C5
Raeburn Infant School *IPSE* IP3 31 H2
Ranelagh Primary School *CHTY* IP2 21 F3
Ransomes Industrial Park *IPSE* IP3 32 D4
Riverside Industrial Park *CHTY* IP2 22 B5
Riverside Theatre & Restaurant *WDBR* IP12 9 G4
Rose Hill Primary School *IPSE* IP3 2
Rushmere Golf Club *IPNE* IP4 2
Rushmere Hall Primary School *IPNE* IP4 1
Rushmere Sports Club *KESG* IP5 1
St Albans Catholic High School *IPNE* IP4 2
St Clements Hospital *IPSE* IP3 2
St Helens Primary School *IPNE* IP4
St Johns CE Primary School *IPNE* IP4 2
St Josephs Prep School & College *CHTY* IP2 2
St Margarets CE Primary School *IP* IP1
St Marks RC Primary School *CHTY* IP2 21
St Marys Catholic Primary School *IPNE* IP4
St Marys CE Primary School *WDBR* IP12
St Marys Primary School *HADL* IP7 37
St Matthews CE Primary School *IP* IP1 2
St Pancras RC Primary School *IP* IP1 11
Sanatorium Felixstowe College *FX* IP11 46
Saracens House Business Centre *IP* IP1 2
Seckford Golf Centre *FRAM/WMKT* IP13 8
Sidegate Primary School *IPNE* IP4 13
Ski Centre *CHTY* IP2 30
Spa Pavillion Theatre *FX* IP11 45
Springbank Industrial Estate *KIR/NAC* IP10 25
Springfield Junior School *IP* IP1 11
Sprites Junior School *CHTY* IP2 29
Sproughton Business Park *IP* IP1 20
Sproughton CE Primary School *RIPW* IP8 20
Stoke County High School *CHTY* IP2 22
Suffolk College *IPNE* IP4 3
The Suffolk Nuffield Hospital at Christchurch Park *IP* IP1 2
Suffolk Retail Park *IP* IP1 21
Suffolk Showground *IPSE* IP3 33
Thomas Wolsey Special School *IP* IP1 11
Thurleston County High School *IP* IP1 11
Tower Ramparts Shopping Centre *IP* IP1 2
Trimley St Martin Primary School *FX* IP11 42
Trimley St Mary Primary School *FX* IP11 43
UGC Cinema *IP* IP1 2
Westbourne High School *IP* IP1 11
Westerfield Business Centre *NHMKT* IP6 12
Whitehouse Industrial Estate *IP* IP1 10
White House J & I School *IP* IP1 11
Whitton Community Primary School *IP* IP1 11
Willis Corroon Building *IP* IP1 2
Wolsey Theatre *IP* IP1 2
Woodbridge Museum *WDBR* IP12 9
Woodbridge Primary School *WDBR* IP12 9
Woodbridge School *WDBR* IP12 9

Notes

QUESTIONNAIRE

Dear Atlas User
Your comments, opinions and recommendations are very important to us. So please help us to improve our street atlases by taking a few minutes to complete this simple questionnaire.

You do NOT need a stamp (unless posted outside the UK). If you do not want to remove this page from your street atlas, then photocopy it or write your answers on a plain sheet of paper.

Send to: The Editor, AA Street by Street, FREEPOST SCE 4598, Basingstoke RG21 4GY

ABOUT THE ATLAS...

Which city/town/county did you buy?

____

Are there any features of the atlas or mapping that you find particularly useful?

____
____
____

Is there anything we could have done better?

____
____
____

Why did you choose an AA Street by Street atlas?

____
____
____

Did it meet your expectations?

Exceeded ☐ **Met all** ☐ **Met most** ☐ **Fell below** ☐

Please give your reasons

____
____
____
____
____

continued overleaf

Where did you buy it?

For what purpose? (please tick all applicable)

To use in your own local area ☐ **To use on business or at work** ☐

Visiting a strange place ☐ **In the car** ☐ **On foot** ☐

Other (please state)

LOCAL KNOWLEDGE...

Local knowledge is invaluable. Whilst every attempt has been made to make the information contained in this atlas as accurate as possible, should you notice any inaccuracies, please detail them below (if necessary, use a blank piece of paper) or e-mail us at *streetbystreet@theAA.com*

ABOUT YOU...

Name (Mr/Mrs/Ms)

Address

Postcode

Daytime tel no

E-mail address

Which age group are you in?

Under 25 ☐ **25-34** ☐ **35-44** ☐ **45-54** ☐ **55-64** ☐ **65+** ☐

Are you an AA member? **YES** ☐ **NO** ☐

Do you have Internet access? **YES** ☐ **NO** ☐

Thank you for taking the time to complete this questionnaire. Please send it to us as soon as possible, and remember, you do not need a stamp (unless posted outside the UK).

ML